KT-468-789

CONTENTS

RESCUE
DOGS
and their second lives

Information, inspiration and practical
support for re-homing a rescue dog

ANGELA PATMORE

ROBINSON

To the dog charities, shelter staff and rescue workers,
and to my dear dog Owen Parsnip

ROBINSON

First published as *Doggerel* in Great Britain in 2010 by Spring Hill,
an imprint of How To Books Ltd

This edition published in 2018 by Robinson

A CIP catalogue record for this book is available from the British Library.

ISBN: 978-1-47213-802-6

Typeset in Arno Pro by SX Composing DTP, Rayleigh, Essex
Printed and bound in Great Britain by CPI Group (UK), Croydon CRO 4YY

Papers used by Robinson are from well-managed forests
and other responsible sources

Robinson
An imprint of
Little, Brown Book Group
Carmelite House
50 Victoria Embankment
London EC4Y 0DZ

An Hachette UK Company
www.hachette.co.uk

www.littlebrown.co.uk

How To Books are published by Robinson, an imprint of Little, Brown Book
Group. We welcome proposals from authors who have first-hand experience of their
subjects. Please set out the aims of your book, its target market and its suggested
contents in an email to Nikki.Read@howtobooks.co.uk

Acknowledgements

I SHOULD VERY much like to thank all the owners and rescue charities who allowed their beloved dogs to be versified in this book. I should also like to thank the following:

Joanna Lumley

Bel Mooney

Annette Crosbie OBE

Jilly Cooper

Sarah Vella-Brown and Oliver Reid, the Greyhound Trust

Adrian Burder and the Dogs Trust

Peter Laurie and the Association of Dogs' and Cats' Homes

Lesley McFadyen, East Anglia Staffordshire Bull Terrier Club

Amy De-Keyzer and the RSPCA

Ceiri O'Douglas, Battersea Dogs and Cats Home

Stephen Cobb and Clarks Farm Greyhound Rescue

Anne Carter and the Labrador Lifeline Trust

Robin Allison-Smith for his photograph of Bonnie
the Maltese Dog

Peter Corns for his photograph of Jasmine

Tessa Codrington for her photograph of Otto

Jon and Anne Hunt, and Dorothy and David Burder,
for their help with research

And finally ...

Publishers Giles Lewis and Nikki Read for believing in
the project.

FOREWORD BY:
JOANNA LUMLEY

IT SEEMS VERY dreadful that the more we become aware of the wretchedness of abandoned dogs, the more frequently they are cruelly treated and discarded, sometimes for simply behaving like the dogs they are.

Angela Patmore's enchanting book has burrowed into the minds of our most loyal friends; her poems are touching, humorous and revealing (I suspect she may have canine genes in her make-up). There are case histories here to jag at your heart, to make you almost ashamed to be human: but the overall impact is of redemption, of wrongs made right by adoption by kind new owners. In her words, in the poem Zak, '. . . A dog can reform. A dog can learn. A dog can be reborn.'

Rescue dogs are often the most rewarding of friends as they are so grateful to have a loving home. They want to please us so that we won't throw them out again. There is usually a reason for a dog being difficult, and it's often man-made. They can be reborn as a good dog with time and care and love. Above all, she captures the entirely different characters and natures of the animals she writes about, because anyone who owns and loves an animal knows that no two are the same, any more than people are.

If I had a wish I would choose to be able to talk to the animals like Doctor Doolittle. I wish I knew what they think of us and why they continue to long for our company. The poet Henry Beston wrote: 'They are not underlings; they are other nations, caught with ourselves in the net of life and time, fellow prisoners of the splendour and travail of the earth.' Maybe by treating animals better we shall ourselves become finer people. After all, a nation is judged by the way it treats its animals. By buying this book you will be helping to unite unwanted animals with the new lives they deserve, loved by new owners, their painful past healed and forgotten.

And perhaps you will even think of adopting a dog yourself: a greater treat I cannot imagine.

Sugar

Sugar is waiting and hoping at DogsTrust Harefield branch in West London, where she arrived as a stray from Surrey Heath Borough Council. Staff say Sugar is 'a sensitive girl who needs a quiet home and someone experienced with powerful breeds that will give her time to settle in. She's wary of new people, especially men, and dislikes formal handling and seeing vets. She would need help with socialisation, but once Sugar knows you she loves nothing more than cuddles.'

I'm big. They may put me in a bag
And dump me out at sea.
Those vets – they stick you with sharp spines.
They tried to poison me.
They gave me pills to shut me up –
I knew too much, could be.
The Council came and caught me
Running round Surrey Heath.
Oh look – there's one of them devil dogs
With the fifty rows of teeth.
Get the snare, mate! Get the lorry!
We'll sling a net on her, don't worry.

Yet I'm a sweet, sweet girl –
Ask anyone who knows me well.
I love a kiss and cuddle.
It's just that I'm in a muddle
With all these shocks and scary men –
I won't let them mess with me again
As I'm a sweet, sweet girl.
I want an owner firm and kind,
An owner who can change my mind
About the human breed.
I'm waiting here with baited breath
So I can lick them half to death.
Big love is what I need.

Bugs

Patterdale Terrier Buggs was rescued six years ago by Alison and Time Clews and now lives 'the life of Riley'. Nobody had wanted her as they thought she was ugly – the vet said her facial injuries were consistent with those of dogs used for badger baiting. Buggs is also deaf (handy for ignoring humans), but her owners say she has learned a few hand signals, 'proving you can teach an old dog new tricks'. Her ode is a tribute from Owen Parsnip, commander-in-chief of Facebook's Dog Revolutionary Army, in which Buggs holds the rank of captain.

Uncommon beauty have I seen in thee
Where first I looked to find a juicy bone:
Thinking no thing could so delicious be,
But now I see my taste in thee alone.
No toothsome morsel can with thee compare
Who art delectable in every part
Nor can I find thy charm in things elsewhere
That once amused me 'ere you won my heart.
Such is the brightness of thy features rare
That over all they carry me away
To realms where woofers ever dream and dare
Since thou hast shown thyself in thine array.
Let pedigree girls strut their vain displays:
None bears the glow that round Buggs' visage plays.

1

I WANT AN UNWANTED DOG

ACCORDING TO THE PDSA's annual Animal Wellbeing (PAW) Report there are now an estimated 9.3 million dogs in the UK along with 11.1 million cats. Among our growing army of pet owners over 4 million did not bother to do any research before they acquired their animal so they knew little about the responsibilities, welfare, training or expense involved. Cats are (controversially) free to roam 24/7 but dogs are much more restricted both by law and by their owners' lifestyles. 465,000 dogs are never walked outside their home or garden. A quarter of the dog population, 2.3 million, are left alone for five hours or more on a weekday. Dog charities advise that this is too long, and that prolonged absence may cause a dog to bark, chew or toilet indoors out of frustration and distress. This in turn leads to abandonment as the animal becomes a nuisance and an inconvenience.

The British public may like to think that, when they abandon their pet dogs by the hundred thousand, they go directly to some sanctuary in the sky where they get free Bonio biscuits and everything is quietly taken care of.

DOG DREGS – THE REALITY

The truth is very different. Here on earth behind the shelter walls, dogs stand in barrack blocks and zinc-lined runs, waiting and hoping, flattening their faces against the bars when they hear human footsteps. And the kennel staff who love them and cannot find them homes get the job of walking the dogs as jauntily as they can and feeding them from charitable donations, or handing them over for their last barbiturate jab – while somewhere far away sit their former owners, blithely oblivious.

Sally, a Battersea girl, belonged to Betty Coppin of Gosfield in Essex, though she was originally spotted at the Dogs' Home by Betty's younger son. She was about six months old, and scared of her own shadow: 'She was thin and very nervous and would not go out at all.' However, Sally took to obedience like a duck to water and won many competitions – on her own terms. 'She had a mischievous streak in her,' says Betty. 'She would not do as bid until she got in the ring and then she would shine.'

In 2015 the Dogs Trust cared for around 17,000 dogs across their 21 rehoming centres. They received 43,771 calls from people trying to give up their dogs. That's 3,647 calls a month or 120 a day. Their latest Stray Dog Survey reveals that 47,596 dogs were heartlessly left behind in council pounds, unclaimed by their owners and each day 280 strays were found wandering and running about the UK. In total 102,363 stray and abandoned dogs were handled by local authorities between 2014 and 2015 and 5,142 of those dogs were destroyed, one dog every two hours.

But these were by no means the only ones put down. Among the animal charities Battersea has a non-selective intake policy. 'This means we take any animal that is in need of our help, regardless of breed, behaviour or medical condition.' They also take what are known as Section One dogs such as Pit Bulls and other banned breeds, 'which we are required by law to hand over to the police to be destroyed under the Dangerous Dogs Act'. Staffies and Staffie crosses made up 28 per cent of their intake. 39 per cent were Bull breeds such as Bull Mastiffs, American Bulldogs and English Bull Terriers. In 2015 Battersea put to sleep 1,389 dogs, 91 of them identified as Section One. The Dangerous Dogs Act does not require a dog to have done any harm for it to be killed. If it resembles a breed considered potentially dangerous, this is sufficient reason for its destruction. The RSPCA has not released a figure for the number of dogs they have euthanised, but the charity has provided the following statement:

> 'The RSPCA rescues the most abused and neglected dogs from heartbreaking situations – starved to the brink of death, burned, stabbed, set on fire, and used to fight each other to the death. Thanks to the dedication and devotion of vets, centre staff, behaviourists and foster carers, thousands of these dogs are nursed back to health, rehabilitated and rehomed every year. However, sadly some have major injuries, health problems and behavioural issues, which means we have to make the difficult decision to put them to sleep to end their suffering. In ninety-nine per cent of cases it is due to veterinary, behavioural or legal reasons or at the owner's insistence. We would urge anyone looking for a dog to think carefully about the responsibility they are taking on and to consider rehoming instead of buying. We would also encourage them to neuter their pets to prevent unplanned litters of puppies.'

Even some of the smaller charities were having up to one third of their dogs euthanised because nobody wanted them, or because they had been unsuitably bred or unsuitably trained, or not trained at all by irresponsible and cruel owners.

One of the reasons regularly given for abandonment is the cost of veterinary treatment, with the hike in VAT to 20% adding to the burden on dog-owners unable to shop around as there are no price comparison websites for this service. Even without expensive vets' bills, the costs of owning and caring for an average-size dog are fairly formidable. The PDSA Report 2015 estimates that over the course of a lifetime it can be anywhere from £16,000 to £31,000 depending on the breed.

THE STRUGGLING SANCTUARIES

Everywhere in Britain, little sanctuaries struggle to survive, for shamefully animal charities receive no state aid and rely entirely on donations. Government contingency plans for dealing with the next rabies outbreak in the UK show how much we take for granted our network of waif-collecting centres and the dedication of a small band of animal lovers fighting to make ends meet. I have visited many of the ADCH shelters listed in this book, and many small unaffiliated shelters that are not listed. The cheerful, kind people who run them do so with little thanks or recognition, day in and day out, working like drudges, often for nothing. They are heroes in every sense and this book is dedicated to them. Why do they do it? I've asked them many a time. They all said the same thing.

'Because the dogs are worth it.'

Animal welfare work in Britain may draw on a huge reservoir of popular sentimentality, but when you actually turn on the tap, a mere trickle comes out. Only a handful of the sympathetic people do anything to help the dedicated few, yet somewhere among the homes and shelters there may be a future friend of yours, pushing his or her snout through the wire netting, thinking perhaps tomorrow you may come.

The dog verses in this book are designed to touch your heart. If they succeed, and you are now considering giving an unwanted dog a place in your home, please make sure that you have thought it through.

THE RIGHT PEOPLE FOR THE RIGHT REASONS

People who decide on a second-hand dog rather than a new puppy usually do so for the best reasons. They have a settled home where dogs are permitted and which isn't about to be disrupted by a move or a new baby. They can afford the food and expensive vets' bills (the PDSA or People's Dispensary for Sick Animals, which offers free treatment in some areas to the genuinely hard-up, is not an animal National Health Service). They have thought about the mess, the exercise, the grooming, the carpets, the garden, the fences and the time and trouble involved in looking after a four-legged friend for maybe ten to fifteen years, and they realise that a dog is more demanding than a cat or a koi carp.

They have thought about the holidays, and what will happen to the dog when they go away, and they've understood that a dog left alone in the house all day while the owners are at work will often show its anxiety and distress by destruction and barking. The whole family

Storm, a three-year-old white Husky, belongs to Jo and Gary Berry and drags them about the streets of Long Melford, Suffolk. They kept seeing her picture on the window of the RSPCA shop in Bury St Edmunds, but Jo had said, 'No more dogs' after they lost their last one. Finally they gave in and went to the RSPCA shelter near Newmarket to see her. The blue eyes did it. Storm was one of three, but she wasn't wanted. Now she's not only wanted but plans to play football for England.

has agreed, including overworked mums and any elderly relatives living at home, that a dog would be welcome, and they have decided where it will be allowed to jump, sit and sleep. And then they have agreed on a rescue dog for its own sake, rather than for what it looks like. They don't just want a fur burglar alarm, a toy or a status symbol. They want a true friend who, once it gets to know its rescuers, will follow them like a shadow, guard them and stand by them through thick and thin.

THE BIG QUESTIONS

So there are a few big questions to ask yourself before you go ahead and adopt a canine waif. The first is: *Do you really want it?* A dog knows no greater anguish than to be abandoned by the owner it loved and a discarded dog has already been through that once. If you think you may be Number Two, please save yourself the trouble.

Secondly, I would advise especial caution if you have young children or grandchildren. Any dog, rescue or not, pure-bred or not, is capable of biting, and small children playing and experimenting with life will often put a pet under the direst pressure while your back is turned. An adult stray from a shelter may have an angelic temperament but it may have been sadistically abused or have ingrained bad habits that will take time and patience to alter. It isn't fair on the child or the dog to expect them to hit it off under these circumstances. Young children cannot read a dog's body language the way grown-ups can. They don't understand where play ends and danger signals begin. This said, many rescue dogs have been successfully homed with children, and the most valuable advice will come from the shelter staff who have had time to get to know the dogs in their care.

There are very few genuinely psychotic dogs that will suddenly bite for no reason at all, but many animals who have suffered great cruelty in the past will snap if they are frightened or pulled about, at least until their confidence in humans is restored. After that you will be able to trust them as you would trust any friend, but do be careful at the outset. Use common sense. The kennel staff will generally know which are the problem customers and they will gladly steer you towards a placid character or a gentle bitch who likes nothing better than kids, kids and yet more kids – as bitches often do. In any case, children must be taught that a dog is not a toy or a squeezebox. Like us, it needs some privacy, rest and respect.

CANINE CASTAWAYS

In 2015 the RSPCA inspectorate collected 1,341 abandoned dogs. They say the peak in admissions occurs in the summer months, especially July. They are not sure why. It may be because the novelty of Christmas puppies has worn off by the summer or because people can't be bothered to make arrangements for their dogs when they go on holiday. It isn't just dogs. They collect on average one animal every hour. 'Every day our inspectors face cases where animals have been left abandoned in fields, dumped in boxes, left for dead at the side of roads and even left outside our animal centres and hospitals. It is heartbreaking,' says an RSPCA spokesperson. Among the dogs discarded like rubbish in 2015 were Bertie the Yorkshire Terrier, dumped with matted fur in a wheelie bin in Essex, Maverick the Staffie abandoned at London Victoria coach station as his owners went on holiday, Peanut the Lurcher puppy left for dead under a bush in Essex, Brodie the Bulldog tied up and dumped outside RSPCA's Harmsworth Hospital and Rose the English Bull Terrier found drowning in a pond. Many of the discarded animals are neglected, weak or desperately ill and in need of medical treatment. Who cares? Do you?

Dogs' lives are evidently not a high priority in the UK and there is no public outcry when yet more shocking figures are published. Another example is that of foxhounds. The foxhunting community do not keep a record of the number of hounds destroyed, but when I queried a report on the radio that between eight and ten thousand were killed annually for being too old or insufficiently agile to do their jobs, the Countryside Alliance told me this was inaccurate and that the figure was 'in the region of three thousand'. Dogs everywhere are being 'got rid of' on an industrial scale and animal charity workers are like people holding out nets at the side of the waterfall, trying to save the ones they can. According to the Dogs Trust Stray Dog Survey, between 1997 (when records began) and 2015 an astounding 2,077,000 UK dogs were classified as 'stray' or abandoned. Admittedly some proportion of these would have been dogs picked up more than once, but the size of the problem is both obvious and staggering.

And this figure does *not* include thousands of unwanted racing greyhounds that simply 'go missing' on a yearly basis rather than get recycled through the Greyhound Trust rescue centres. Many of these ex-racers, as rescue campaigners know, have been very cruelly disposed of, and ten thousand bodies were illegally buried in a landfill site in County Durham. A frequent method of execution is with a gun or a bolt-gun. The Greyhound Clinic, Ockendon Kennels in Upminster, offers £30 a head for healthy greyhounds that can be killed for body parts for research, and the trade is condoned by the Royal Veterinary College (I have statements to this effect).

Other canine cast-offs were dropped from bridges, on motorways, in rivers and wheelie-bins – ex-pets, door-mutts, surplus to requirements. Animal welfare workers, sickened by the rising tide, plead for changes in the law and save as many as they can. Still the animal-loving British public rush out to buy more dogs, new dogs, expensive dogs, and the flourishing dog trade produces litter after litter, selling them on the internet to anyone with sufficient cash. The shelters, already bursting at the seams, squeeze in a few more, putting two and even three to a cage, until there is simply no more room at the inn.

During a recession people throw out their dogs like old shoes to save money, so this book has been written to focus people's minds on this emergency and what it really means. Waifs and strays that cannot be found room for end up in vans bound for the local vet's or agency kennels where they have a few days' grace before being quietly destroyed, never to trouble the animal-loving British public again.

PUPPY FARMS

Those wary of adopting a rescue dog point out that there are risks involved, and this is true. But there are also risks in purchasing a new pup, and one of these is the growing international problem of puppy farming. Pressure groups like Pups Not Profit and Pet Abuse UK campaign against heartless dog farmers. Their websites make truly alarming reading. Pups kept in cramped, coffin-like conditions, or kept in the dark, sick and frightened. 'Commodity' sellers bringing in crates from abroad containing poorly and desperate pups that stand little chance of health or happiness. Greedy breeders turning over fast profits by churning out bloated and dying little fashion breeds to unsuspecting members of the public hoping to buy a 'safe' pet for their children. Campaigning groups go after the puppy farmers and try to bring them to justice, but new operations spring up in sheds and barns along quiet lanes all over the country. They are very difficult to police.

The Kennel Club is understandably worried about all this because it brings dog breeding into disrepute. They tell purchasers to proceed with caution. They advise those looking to buy a pup to go to a responsible and reputable Kennel Club Assured Breeder and ask to see the puppy's mother. They tell them to look at the kennelling conditions, and to ask to see the relevant health certificates for the puppy's parents. They say to be suspicious of a breeder selling different breeds and not to buy a puppy from a pet shop. They warn buyers not to pick up the puppy from a neutral location such as a car park or motorway service station. They say: 'Don't buy a puppy because you feel like rescuing it. You'll only be making space available for another poorly pup to fill and condemning further puppies to a miserable life.'

On the Kennel Club website, they advise anyone with suspicions about an unscrupulous breeder to contact the police, the RSPCA or their local authority. And they tell pup buyers: 'If somebody who you suspect of being a puppy farmer is registering their dogs with the Kennel Club, then ensure that you tell the Kennel Club about your suspicions. The Kennel Club would never knowingly register puppies from a puppy farmer and will tell the relevant authorities to try and ensure that the person is brought to book.'

The Kennel Club does indeed offer encouragement to people who might prefer a rescue dog anyway, and they publish a directory of their own breed rescue organisations. Information on how to contact these excellent groups is mentioned in our directory section. But the Secretary of the Kennel Club, Caroline Kisko (in an article about dog-stealing) makes a rather different statement that must concern us. She said, in the *Daily Mail* in June 2016, that generally what she called 'second-hand' dogs had no actual value, but that when a breed becomes popular or fashionable people will pay high prices for the trendy pups. She also expressed the view that insufficient breeding in the UK has created a market for dogs that have either been stolen or bred in foreign puppy farms.

'Generally second-hand dogs have no real value but, because of popularity, a breed can carry a perceived value which people will pay for because they want to be part of the trend ... There is not enough breeding in this country, which means there is space to sell dogs that have been stolen or bred in puppy farms abroad.'

I happen to strongly disagree with both parts of this statement. Second-hand dogs are extremely precious and those who think otherwise, as Oscar Wilde puts it in *Lady Windermere's Fan*, 'know the price of everything and the value of nothing'. And I hope this whole book bears testimony to the inaccuracy of the second part of this statement.

Before you go out and buy a new dog, please come to any of the nation's ADCH shelters and look at their second-hand rows. Whether or not you meet a friend, it will bring home to you the enormity of the problem throughout the UK, and the callousness with which other people have shrugged off their responsibilities. You will see faces to amuse you, faces to accuse you and, if you have any feelings at all, faces to break your heart. In the words of the Dogs Trust's famous slogan, *A dog is for life, not just for Christmas*.

Laddie

Laddie was supposed to be 'about seven' when Dot Burder took him home from Willow Tree Animal Sanctuary in Essex where she was a volunteer helper. In fact he was about twelve. He looked at her with very squinny little eyes and made a strange pleading squeak, which won Dot over. Devoted to her and her son David he went to training classes and gained some confidence but he has always been a nervous, sensitive fellow.

'Help me!' says Laddie: 'That bowl is a bother –
It's either too low or too high.
That room where they set my grub down is another.
Supposed to be safe – that's a lie.
You're lapping your drink and hear clanging from hell
As a sudden spoon falls to the floor.
I worry when walking on lino as well as
I could slip-slide straight through the door.
So I back out of there with unusual care
And I hide in the garden or tear up the stair
As I just cannot take any more.
Not every Rough Collie's like Lassie, a dare-all.
Forget raging rivers and fire.
I never yet rescued a person in peril:
I might try - but then I might tire!
I'm deaf, truth to tell, and I can't see that well
Plus my teeth are now missing or brown.
If it weren't for my owner I'd be like that Jonah.
Some great woe would swallow me down.'

2

WHERE TO FIND ONE

IF YOU DECIDE on a rescue dog rather than a new pedigree or fashionable crossbred puppy, you are literally saving a dog's life, because even if the one you choose is not itself on death row, you will be making room at the shelter for another waif who may well have just days to live. Many overcrowded shelters are forced to destroy inmates after the statutory seven days, and now that responsibility for impounding strays has shifted from the police to local authorities, lost souls are kept for the week at council-appointed agencies before being put to sleep. Most of the dogs locked up on death row have committed no crime, and there are many affecting cases of animals pleading, in their doggie ways, to live. One mongrel about to be put down at Battersea sat up on his haunches and begged with his paws together. He was reprieved by staff, but few are so lucky. Nobody wants them.

The ADCH (Association of Dogs and Cats Homes) is the umbrella organisation that embraces many of the UK and

Southern Ireland's animal charities, shelters and re-homing centres up and down the British Isles. In the list in Appendix 2 you will see all the member charities with their phone numbers and email addresses so you can find one or two with branches near you. You can also go on the ADCH website (www.adch.org.uk) for more at-a-glance information. There are many hundreds of ADCH centres and although we have listed many, it would be impractical to try to print all their branch details in this book. Rest assured, there is a centre not far away!

Even if you already know the shelter address do please ring them up or go on their website before you visit, as many animal charities depend on volunteer staff and they are all extremely busy (you might even, if you have any time to spare, consider giving them a hand – they would be desperately grateful). Some of the larger organisations have branches all over the UK, but if you contact any of the listed member charities by phone or visit their websites you can locate a shelter near you and may even be able to see pictures of their dogs currently waiting for homes.

BATTERSEA DOGS & CATS HOME

Battersea Dogs & Cats Home was founded in 1860 and aims to never turn away a dog or cat in need of help, caring for them until their owners or loving new homes can be found, no matter how long it takes. We are champions for and supporters of vulnerable dogs and cats, determined to create lasting changes for animals in our society. We take care of over eight thousand dogs and cats every year across three sites: one in the beautiful Kent countryside location of Brands Hatch, another in historic Old Windsor in Berkshire, and of course our iconic south London site in Battersea. Our centres are open every day and welcome visitors to come and meet us and the animals in need of new homes.

Alice had spent the first three years of her life in a shed and was very nervous and shy when Cindy and Tony Hilling acquired her from one of the Retired Greyhound Trust branches for whom Cindy works as a home checker. Now Alice is thriving. She shares Cindy and Tony's Essex home with Lurcher Bracken and twelve other beloved rescue Greyhounds – many of them, like Alice, the victims of past cruelty.

From the moment we welcomed our first stray dog in 1860, we have been placing our animals at the centre of everything we do. More than three million animals later, we're still working hard to achieve our vision that every dog and cat should live in a home where they are treated with love, care and respect. Since it was founded, Battersea has rescued, reunited and re-homed over 3.1 million dogs and cats. We care for an average of 260 dogs and 220 cats across our three centres at any one time.

Battersea operates a non-selective intake policy. This means that we will take any animal in need of help, irrespective of breed, medical condition or behaviour. As a result, we regularly receive pets with serious medical conditions and/or behavioural problems. This puts the onus on our dedicated clinical team and Canine

Welfare and Behavioural experts to ensure each animal is assessed and treated on a case-by-case basis and to do the best we possibly can to give them the best possible chance of a happy future.

Every dog and cat that comes into the Home is treated with compassion and dignity and is assessed by a member of our Veterinary team and highly experienced and trained behavioural assessors.

One of the large Hilling family of rescue greyhounds, Jody came originally from the village of Gestingthorpe in Essex. Cindy Hilling explains: 'Her owner had died in his bungalow and when they were found Jody was sitting with him, waiting for him to wake up. Jody came to us at four years of age. She is a steady, easy girl to look after and very well behaved.' Jody is also very photogenic and knows it. She likes to sit in armchairs posing and fluttering her eyelashes.

If, after assessment, the animal is suitable for re-homing we will care for that animal for as long as it takes for the right owner to be found. In some cases this can take a matter of days but for others it may be many months before they finally find the perfect new home.

Battersea Dogs & Cats Home receives no central government funding towards the care of its dogs and cats and relies on the generosity and support of the public to help care for lost and abandoned animals. For further information on Battersea Dogs & Cats Home please visit www.battersea.org.uk

With your support we can help the eight thousand dogs and cats that come into our care. Donate now.

Battersea Dogs & Cats Home
4 Battersea Park Road
London
SW8 4AA
T: 0843 509 4444

THE BLUE CROSS

Sick, injured and homeless pets have relied on Blue Cross since 1897. Abandoned or unwanted, ill or injured, pets turn to them for help every year. Their doors are always open to them, and with the support of animal lovers, they always will be.

Each year, thousands of cats, dogs, small pets and horses turn to Blue Cross animal hospitals, clinics and re-homing services for treatment and to find them the happy homes they deserve.

The charity's **vision** is that every pet will enjoy a healthy life in a happy home and they won't rest until they achieve it.

Blue Cross finds homes for thousands of unwanted cats, dogs, small pets and horses across the UK every year. Their tailor-made service means they help each pet find the right person for them.

Find out more at www.bluecross.org.uk

CLARKS FARM GREYHOUND RESCUE

Clarks Farm Greyhound Rescue
Wash Lane, Maldon CM9 8LX
Phone: 01621 788315

We started with a small rescue centre at Brentwood in Essex with just a few dogs, and when we moved from there we bought a derelict farmyard with outbuildings in September 1999. We had the vision of a 'one-stop shop' for greyhounds and, after many battles with Maldon council, in 2003 we were granted permission for a kennel block with twenty-six purpose-built kennels. After that we applied for kitchen facilities: a greyhound kitchen, visitors' kitchen and toilets etc, and once these were granted we were well on our way to achieving our goal.

We had an old barn that was falling down and thought what a wonderful idea it would be to have our own on-site greyhound vet, because most days we were taking greyhounds many miles to be neutered and this was taking up much of our time. So once again we approached Maldon council. They agreed it would be of great benefit, so in 2010 our state-of-the-art greyhound veterinary surgery became operational.

We were designated a branch of the Greyhound Trust in 2002, and in 2007 became the official homing centre for ex-Crayford racers. We now have many volunteers who work their socks off doing shows and raising general awareness of the benefits of owning a lovely greyhound. We also have an annual September show to highlight greyhounds, but all breeds are welcome and many of them come.

> 'How did we find Sam? We saw a sad photograph in the paper. A sad-looking old dog, and a very sad story told by the staff at the rescue centre at Martlesham Heath. But a happy ending when Sam came to live with us. We only had eleven months with this dear old chap but they were eleven joyous months, and his spirit still roams the cottage and the garden.' – Jon and Anne Hunt, Gosfield in Essex.

In 2009 an adorable black greyhound came in and, as we always do with our dogs once they are neutered, we checked that he was OK with other breeds, particularly little ones. This lad was great and he passed a cat test as well. He went home to a young family and was doing fine; in fact he became a star with the local school.

Then out of the blue we got a phone call from Sky TV. It turned out that they had been following this greyhound 'from puppy to track' and now they wanted to update his progress. We told them he had been homed, and after a few phone calls it was agreed that Sky would film his story, following a day with his family and the work of Clarks Farm on TV. This programme was a wonderful boost for greyhounds, showing just how quickly they settle into life after the track.

Having lost many pet greyhounds ourselves, we were asked by other owners if we could provide a respectful service for them to be laid to rest when they pass. So we have built a cremation centre with a lovely chapel of rest and memorial garden. We call it Rainbows Rest, and it has helped so many people. Each greyhound comes home to a place where that dog can be safe and whole for eternity.

Stephen Cobb

THE DOGS TRUST

Founded in 1891, Dogs Trust is the UK's largest dog welfare charity. Every year we care for over fifteen thousand dogs at our network of twenty-one re-homing centres. It is fundamental to our ethos that no healthy dog in our care is ever destroyed. We're passionate about our four-legged friends, and we're striving to bring about the day when no dog in the UK or Ireland is put to sleep for want of a loving home.

Samantha is one of the abused greyhounds rescued by the Greyhound Trust and subsequently given a home by the greyhound-loving Hillings of Essex. Samantha, who came originally from Lincolnshire, stole the author's heart the moment she met her. Once you have made friends she craves affection and just hates it when you leave. Says Cindy Hilling: 'She has settled down really well but she is still anxious around people she doesn't know and she is inclined to pull on the lead.'

At any one time, Dogs Trust has around 1,500 dogs at our centres. We always endeavour to find the perfect match between dog and adopter and offer free advice for life after our dogs have found their forever homes. Our dogs are fully vaccinated, neutered, wormed and vet-checked before they go home. We also provide four weeks of free Petplan insurance and can offer dog training classes at most of our centres.

Our re-homing centres are welcoming places with everything our dogs need to keep them happy before they leave us. Most of all, all our canine residents receive all the love and care they need (and deserve) from our dedicated staff.

We have re-homing centres at Ballymena, Basildon, Bridgend, Canterbury, Darlington, Dublin, Evesham, Glasgow, Harefield (West London), Ilfracombe, Kenilworth, Leeds, Loughborough, Manchester, Merseyside, Newbury, Salisbury, Shoreham by Sea, Shrewsbury, Snetterton and West Calder.

You can find out more about our centres and how to re-home a Dogs Trust dog by visiting www.dogstrust.org.uk. Or you could simply pop into your local centre to find out more.

As well as re-homing, we aim to tackle the root causes of dog abandonment through youth education, microchipping and neutering campaigns. We also give veterinary treatments to dogs belonging to homeless people and assist dog-owning families who are fleeing domestic violence.

Dogs Trust is a registered charity and receives no government funding. If you would like to make a donation, please visit our website. Any gift will be gratefully received.

THE KENNEL CLUB BREED RESCUE
The Kennel Club breed rescue organisations re-home approximately sixteen thousand dogs each year. Our commitment to rescue continues to grow as we work ever more closely with breed

rescue to support the work that is done to find the right homes for purebred dogs in the UK. Breed rescue organisations have specialist knowledge about their particular breeds and can advise on the type of environment and care that the dogs require.

For over thirty years the Kennel Club has published a rescue directory to list the many general and breed rescue organisations that exist around the country. This has proved to be a useful tool for anyone looking to adopt a dog or wanting to re-home a pet. The rescue directory is a valuable source of information for the general public, veterinary surgeries, dog wardens, police, dog clubs and other welfare organisations. Please contact pam.hill@thekennelclub.org.uk if you would like a copy of the directory.

The Kennel Club advises that anyone considering giving a home to a rescue dog should make sure they are prepared to put in extra work if it is needed, and that this can be an immensely rewarding experience. The Kennel Club's 'Find a Rescue Dog' online service provides contact details for breed rescue organisations for your chosen pedigree dog breed by area. Please visit http://www.thekennelclub.org.uk/services/public/findarescue/Default.aspx to use this service.

Kennel Club Breed Rescue is supported by the Kennel Club Charitable Trust, which offers financial assistance to many dog welfare programmes throughout the UK. Each year they create a Breed Rescue calendar, which for each month features a different dog that has been re-homed by a Kennel Club Breed Rescue organisation. The calendar is a great opportunity to raise funds for Kennel Club Breed Rescue and helps the Kennel Club to promote and support breed rescue organisations across the country in any way they can. The calendar is available to purchase through the online shop http://www.thekennelclubshop.org.uk/products/breed-rescue-calendar

MANCHESTER AND CHESHIRE DOGS' HOMES

Manchester and Cheshire Dogs' Homes (www.dogshome.net, tel: 0844 504 1212) are two local institutions under one fantastic charity.

Manchester Dogs' Home in Harpurhey, North East Manchester, was founded in the 19th century by local philanthropists who wanted to care for abandoned dogs in the city. It has cared for vulnerable dogs across Manchester and beyond for over a hundred years and is truly a much-loved local institution.

Having suffered a devastating arson attack in September 2014 in which dozens of its dogs perished, the Dogs' Home is now back doing what it does best – giving dogs a great second chance in life – and a three-year rebuild is under way. The rebuild, which has only been possible thanks to an incredible outpouring of public support, incorporates the very latest thinking in dog welfare to make the new kennels as dog-friendly as possible.

Kennel sponsorship is available at Manchester Dogs' Home, as are dog sponsorship schemes. The Dogs' Home also operates a comprehensive programme of outreach work including puppy behaviour classes, microchipping clinics and discounted neutering and spaying. The Home Manager at the Manchester site is Steve Mapley.

Sister site Cheshire Dogs' Home in Grappenhall near Warrington is a state-of-the-art facility with a bespoke canine maternity unit, specialist 'respite kennels' for dogs struggling to adapt to kennels life and an off-road woodland walk where a dedicated team of volunteers walk the resident dogs.

Cheshire Dogs' Home is much loved in the local community and runs very popular annual events including the Summer Fair, Sponsored Walk, Spooky Woodland Walk, Christmas Fair and Animal Blessing. Sponsorship opportunities and stalls are available at all the Home's events. Kennel sponsorship is available all year round. The Home Manager at the Cheshire site is Anna Stansfield.

Together, the Dogs' Homes re-home an incredible 94 per cent of all the dogs that come through their doors.

THE MAYHEW ANIMAL HOME

Since 1886, The Mayhew Animal Home has been one of the most effective animal welfare charities in London, helping thousands of dogs and cats to escape a life of abandonment, cruelty and neglect every year. We help animals in need gain a better quality of life through our animal care, community education and welfare projects, working with pet owners and helping the vulnerable, sick and elderly take care of their pets.

The Mayhew takes in and looks after hundreds of unwanted and neglected animals every year, re-homing them with responsible and caring owners. We keep dogs and cats in our care until they are re-homed, for as long as it takes. In 2015 we rehomed 542 cats and dogs and our Animal Welfare Officer team helped 1,327 animals in the community.

The Mayhew has helped rescue animals like Labrador and Collie cross Ben, an emaciated dog who had been passed around between several owners, but who has finally found happiness at his new home. When our Animal Welfare Officers first discovered the ten-year-old, he was emaciated, unable to use his back legs which had collapsed due to muscle weakness, and living in poor conditions. But three months later, with the help of Mayhew Officers, staff and vets, Ben was transformed into a healthy, happy dog and even landed himself a loving forever home.

We also helped rescue four young, unwanted puppies aged two to three months. The four pups – two females and two males named by staff as Moe, Sandy, Tom and Jimmy – were unfortunately bred for purely commercial reasons. When they were left unsold, they were no longer wanted, so our Animal Welfare Officers rescued them and brought them into the care of our Home. All four pups have now found happiness in their new forever homes.

We take care of cats and dogs for as long as it takes for us to find them their new home. Not every animal in our care can find their dream straight away, but at The Mayhew we provide a fostering scheme and are always looking for more dedicated foster carers to help us look after our animals. Although The Mayhew's accommodation is fabulously comfy and homely, some animals simply don't cope well in a rescue environment. In this kind of situation it's much nicer for an animal to have a temporary home instead. Fostering also frees up space at The Mayhew for other animals in need of our care.

To find out more about The Mayhew's work, visit www.themayhew.org

For adoption and general enquiries, call: 0208 962 8000. To donate, call: 0208 206 5870.

THE GREYHOUND TRUST

The Greyhound Trust (GT) is a national charity founded in 1975. Since then it is proud to have found over seventy-five thousand loving homes for greyhounds. Each year, they home approximately four thousand retired racing greyhounds and help hundreds more, making it the country's largest single-breed re-homing charity.

The charity strives for a day when all racing greyhounds retire to loving homes and are treated with compassion and kindness.

The Trust promotes re-homing and works with those involved in greyhound racing, helping to raise the profile of the thousands of greyhounds retiring from the sport each year. GT also liaises with other canine welfare charities to find good homes for greyhounds across Britain.

GT has a network of over sixty branches, each run by volunteers. Funding comes only through the generosity of the general public and from the greyhound racing industry.

If you would like to find out more about the Greyhound Trust, or wish to support the charity, please visit www.greyhoundtrust.org.uk

RSPCA

We are the RSPCA. We prevent cruelty; we promote kindness; we alleviate suffering; we rescue and re-home; we care and nurture; we are here for all animals, for life.

When the RSPCA was founded in a London coffee shop in 1824, it became the world's first animal welfare charity. Since then, our staff and volunteers have been working tirelessly towards our goal – to create a world in which all humans respect and live in harmony with members of the animal kingdom. We believe every animal has the right to be treated as an individual.

Our inspectors and officers rescue animals from the most unimaginable cruelty and neglect, and our centre staff and veterinary professionals focus on rehabilitating and re-homing these animals or releasing wildlife back into the countryside. Behind the scenes, our staff investigate cruelty complaints and the prosecution team seek to take the most serious cases to court, while scientists work on research, information and advice to help people care for their pets in the best possible way and to improve welfare standards for all animals. The public affairs department seeks opportunities to update and improve legislation so it better protects animals, and also lobbies the government for change to make this country a better place for all animals – including pets, farm animals, wildlife and animals used in research laboratories.

We are the voice for those who have no voice. We work to bring about change to protect animals today and in the future; we rescue animals from heartbreaking situations and are dedicated to rehabilitating and re-homing as many as possible; and we pledge to speak up for those who cannot speak themselves.

You can't buy love, but you can rescue it. And that's what the RSPCA has done, 24 hours a day, 365 days a year, for 192 years.

WOOD GREEN, THE ANIMALS' CHARITY
From humble beginnings in 1924, Wood Green, The Animals' Charity has grown to become one of the leading animal welfare organisations in the UK.

We take in animals of all shapes and sizes! As well as cats and dogs, we find loving new homes for thousands of chickens, rabbits, mice, guinea pigs, goats, sheep, ferrets and more!

We think owning an animal is one of the most rewarding things you can do, and we are here to offer help and support to both people and their pets.

OUR VISION IS OF A WORLD WHERE ALL PETS ARE WELL CARED FOR IN LOVING HOMES FOR LIFE.

WE AIM TO ACHIEVE THIS VISION BY:

- Providing the best possible care for animals in need.

- Promoting good animal welfare and responsible pet ownership by providing support, guidance and education to members of the public.

- Setting standards of animal welfare in the UK and beyond.

WE SEEK TO WORK IN PARTNERSHIP WITH THOSE WHO SHARE OUR VISION.

OUR VALUES:

- We aim to find the right home for every animal in our care.

- We endeavour to support anyone who needs help caring for their pets.

- We believe the emotional and physical well-being of every animal we look after is paramount.

- We are proud of our non-judgmental and compassionate approach.

- We value our volunteers, staff, supporters and partners.

- We pride ourselves on being open, honest and committed in every aspect of our work.

OUR MISSION:
To take in unwanted and lost animals, provide shelter and care, find secure and loving homes, provide advice, support and guidance for pet owners, and increase the public's awareness of its responsibility towards animals in society.

Each animal that comes through our doors is assessed by our experienced team, and our aim is to ensure that the right home is found for every animal.

Our centres for re-homing are open to the public seven days a week (including Bank Holidays) – visit woodgreen.org.uk to find out more about Wood Green, The Animals' Charity.

Alvin

In November 2009 Lorraine and Peter Eyles visited Albery Dog Rescue in Bedfordshire run by an ex-vet called Joy. Among the dogs they saw, recalls Lorraine, was 'a very anxious' Alvin. 'We had had no experience with a strong-willed Bull Terrier, but he was a very stable, friendly, curious little chap. He gets on well with other dogs and has many girlfriends, including a Labradoodle named Barley, twice his size. Despite being bitten by little dogs Alvin has never once retaliated. He is truly an ambassador for his breed.'

Bundle of nerves and desperate to please:
Dumped on a Portsmouth street.
Squirmed in a small cage for a year.
Scar on his lip, and limps a bit.
Humans have been hard on his breed.
What did these ones need, or fear?
Should he look fierce, fight, compete?
Or should he give these his love?
If he guessed right they might take him along.
If not, like thousands more
He'd go through that trap door
Where all the Staffies go
Who try to please and just guess wrong.
We took him for a long walk on the lead:
Noticed some crossing to avoid him.
Alvin the joyous, keen to meet and greet.
First night in the dark, snuffled and peed.
Searched under our king-size bed.
We felt the earth move – that was Alvin's head
Shifting the weight. Still, 'from the strong
Cometh forth sweetness' – and an apelike song:
Mewlings and strange growlings.
Yet when the carol singers came
Feeling utterly out of his depth
Alvin wet himself on our step.
Up for a bundle with the lads,
Gentle with women, kind to kids.
Sitting oddly on his bum
Crossing his bandy legs – The Geezer –
Belly protruding like a beery tum:
Look at our Monkey – made of sterling stuff
Loyal and loving. We'd have fifty like him.
Give them a chance, this breed so feared, derided:
Could be those anti–Alvins are misguided.

Jo

The author's big blue ex-racer Jo came from the Clarks Farm branch of the Greyhound Trust at Little Totham in Essex, where staff have actually re-homed a thousand other cast-off racers. Jo had eight wins at Catford before he was lamed and discarded. To the shelter staff he was known as 'G.O.G.' (Grumpy Old Git) for nipping dog bottoms or tails that poked through his cage. But he was recuperating from a broken leg and besides, he was very aristocratic. Yes, the embarrassing incident described on page 33 actually happened, and Jo is pictured just after his accomplishment.

A fine tenth birthday I'd get: You'd think they'd have a care.

You're not ten very often, and even then it's rare.

They'd take me somewhere surely where dogs can romp and roam:

A seashore or a meadow, a disused aerodrome.

No – Glastonbury Abbey. What larks I should have there.

A fossil with no meat on, a dark and dogless prayer.

We waddled to our picnic: 'ALL DOGS ON LEADS' it said.

This called for concentration: a sharp jerk of my head

Then collar off and bingo! Around that place I tore:

Legs going like the clappers, lungs billowing for more.

I did a princely circuit, a round-the-ruins race.

I felt I'd done a good job, and livened up the place.

They think I'm not religious, but who could truly say

The spirit wasn't on me, when I was ten that day?

3
PRACTICALITIES

HOW MUCH DOES IT COST?

So far as costs are concerned, the rescue dog is a bargain. Not only do most British dogs' homes check the animal's health and temperament for you, but they will take back any dog that proves unsuitable. You won't get a fairer deal than that from a pedigree breeder.

How much do the shelters charge? It varies from a suitable donation to a couple of hundred pounds (again you can get this information by ringing the charity itself). Many animal homes run on a shoestring and must therefore ask you to help with 'the ones left behind'. Besides, these dogs have already been cast off once as valueless. If they were simply given away free, what chance of the same thing happening again? Compare what these charities ask with what breeders may charge you for a puppy

– anything up to £1,500 and even beyond – and you get some idea what a good deal this is.

Sometimes the charity officially retains ownership of the dog, should anything unforeseen happen to prevent you from looking after it in the future. Some of the larger charities are able to run a visiting system, with someone to give advice, do a home check and see how the new family member is settling in. Inexperienced dog owners find this a tremendous help, although not all shelters can afford to do it.

DISEASES AND VACCINATION

Some people who write pedigree dog books are fond of warning readers not to adopt a rescue dog. They say these 'rejects' must be either dangerous or diseased and that you should only ever get a puppy from a pedigree breeder. *Rubbish!* say all the owners of our rescue dogs. Getting a waif from a shelter has brought as much joy and love to the rescuers as spending a king's ransom on a pure-bred puppy. As to the risk of disease, all the larger charity shelters I've visited gave their dogs a medical check-up before they let them out and vaccinated them against the major diseases. Those with manageable numbers even wormed, bathed and deflea-ed them as well. There is always the chance of infection between animals crowded together, whether it be in a fastidious shelter, a show or a vet's waiting room, and staff at dogs' homes realise the risks and take every possible precaution, watching for signs of incubated disease on their premises. Canine parvovirus broke out, not in these charity homes, but at pedigree shows and kennels.

Please take your new adopted dog, whether pup or adult, to the local vet and he or she will advise you on vaccination for your area, but phone beforehand, explaining where the animal comes from and roughly how old it is. If it's a puppy, it should be carried or taken by car; if it's an adult and too big to carry, the vet will advise you on the phone what to do. In these circumstances some prefer to make a house call, to save you walking the streets with an uninoculated dog and sitting in their waiting room. (If you don't know of a local vet, look on the internet or in the Yellow Pages.) All dogs need protection against the killer diseases and the larger rescue organisations will arrange initial vaccination themselves. Survival of the fittest is all very well unless your particular dog happens not to be the fittest, and you should be on his or her side should nature call them to account. Never take an uninoculated dog out and about until its vaccination is complete. A puppy is utterly vulnerable and an adult dog transported to a new area runs a high risk of infection. Rescue dogs are not expensive. The least you can do is to pay for a course of vaccination for the poor little devil.

The major dog killers in the UK are distemper (and hardpad), infectious canine hepatitis (also known as viral hepatitis and nothing to do with the human version), leptospirosis and canine parvovirus. Distemper, a frequently fatal viral disease, is signalled early on by fever, listlessness and lack of appetite, as well as vomiting. These signs may be followed by coughing, yellow discharge from the nose and eyes, thickening of the skin and footpads, and convulsions. The disease is airborne and even if a dog recovers, he may have infected other dogs and be left with incurable tremors all his life. A couple of jabs will see your dog or puppy through all these dangerous diseases for the first year and thereafter you should consult your vet on the necessity of boosters. Some authorities now question the need for top-up vaccinations and research has emerged on certain health risks associated with them. Please do your homework and find out about this – as the dog's owner it will be your responsibility and finally your decision.

Canine hepatitis is a liver disease; leptospirosis has two forms, one of which attacks the kidneys; and canine parvovirus (the name means 'little virus') is a comparatively new form of enteritis that can kill without showing any symptoms at all. In North America and the European continent, of course, rabies vaccination is required by law, and now that we can take dogs abroad with a pet passport, canine globetrotters must get their shots just like human travellers. When I was visiting the shelters researching my other dog books (I've written five earlier ones), pups in kennels and shelters would often, to save expense, be given a 'measles' vaccination against distemper to tide them over. You should ask about this and whether you may have a certificate for your vet's reference.

> Dudley belongs to Mandy Little, managing director of literary agents Watson Little in London. While not exactly on the staff, he is on the website, so feels entitled to spend his days 'scavenging and squeezing plastic squeaky toys' while people are trying to work. He came from Sutton Coldfield at the age of four via a website called PreLoved, and settled in very quickly. Dudley lists his hobbies as 'innovative fiction and pinching tuna sandwiches'.

Vaccination will cost you something (the PDSA do *not* offer it free). But you should think of this as part of the purchase price of your pet.

CHOOSING ONE TO SUIT YOU

Of course you don't have to choose *one* at all: two that have been kennelled together may be lifelong pals and will often help each other settle in. If they are of opposite sexes, of course, one would need to be neutered, and you should also think in terms of which dog will be 'in charge': animals are not democratic and if there is any doubt about their status they tend to fight. A difference in size or age will help them make up their minds.

The choice of pup or adult, male or female, large or small, smooth or shaggy, will depend entirely on you and your family set-up. What can you handle? The most popular choices *are the easiest to re-home*. The more unlovely, scraggy, elderly and miserable a dog looks, the slimmer its chances of impressing anyone. It will probably skulk in the corner or stare out from its plastic bed, knowing its doggie days are numbered. If you don't have children, you might consider one of these despondent wrecks. They may not like you at all at first; they may not eat; they may hide behind the sofa. But as you can see from the doggies herein versed, they can come out like stars and bluebells, with a little patience.

PUPS

Pups are notoriously cuddly. This is a trick of nature to get you to take them home, where they will go through a wetting and messing stage, followed by a teething and tearing stage. Try to look at the pup as a would-be dog and you'll get the picture. It may be intending to grow into something unusual, and today's large-footed babe may be tomorrow's behemoth. Rescue pups are often kennelled with their mother, so you can see at least half of what you'll get.

Pups have a socialising period between four and fourteen weeks, and the ideal time to adopt is around seven to nine weeks. Before that, they need contact with their littermates or they may grow up unsure of other dogs, and if it's later, they may have problems adjusting to people. A pup should be picked up carefully, using both hands, and cradled gently. Many dog tots are badly injured by being dropped, and children are often the droppers. A healthy pup is wriggly, soft and plump. Its skin is loose and mobile and flops back into place. There should be no discharge from eyes or nose: frothy milk down the nose may be a sign of a cleft palate. Coughs and sneezes indicate more than a cold, and pop-eyes are a bad sign too. Ears should be clean and not smelly; teeth should clench perfectly and gums should be pink, not anaemic-looking. Little thighs should be free from spots and scabs; black specs in the fur mean flea-dirt, and signs of diarrhoea mean trouble. Tums should have no lumps or bumps: umbilical hernias require a minor operation. Limbs should be strong rather than rickety. Beware of adopting a cold, skinny pup, unless you are prepared for it to die on you.

Another of the Hilling Hounds, Eva is a small, muscly girl with a funny run and black, glossy coat. I hear that black greyhounds are known in certain racing circles as 'dustbin bags' because there are so many of them and they are easily disposed of. Eva is extremely beautiful. She is cuddly with humans but enjoys trying to boss the rest of the household's dogs about, notwithstanding Alpha female Kesha. Eva came from the Greyhound Trust and was born on 11 May 2004.

A bloated appearance, though, simply means worms, and you should have the puppy wormed by a vet in any case. Roundworms such as toxocara canis (about which we have all heard so much) look like pieces of pinkish cotton or string, 5 to 15 cm long and coiled like a spring. They may cause coughing, vomiting and diarrhoea in pups, and the eggs may cause an extremely rare disease called toxocariasis in children if they ingest infected soil. Tell children to wash their hands after playing with pups (or soil) and make sure your pet is given appropriate doses of worming tablets from the vet.

There is another common parasite found in dogs – the tapeworm, which is flat like a piece of tape and attaches to the dog's bowel by little stickers. Small segments like rice grains or melon seeds break off and are deposited on the ground. Tapeworms are usually associated with one of their hosts, the flea, so if you see signs of either ask the vet to prescribe a little something. Tapeworms may cause listlessness and loss of appetite in a pup but may be symptomless. Parasitic worms, by the way, are common in mammals. Cats have their own and so do we – threadworms, found in children, are nothing to do with pets.

ADULTS

Rescue dogs of all ages come in every shape and size. Age can be roughly determined by tooth discolouration, although this may also be due to illness. Yellowish brown stains and bluntness of the canines usually mean the dog is over five years old, unless it smokes a pipe. Dogs do go grey like humans, in their case around the muzzle, and older dogs lose their figures too. Please don't write off critters past their first flush of youth. They still have a lot of mileage in them, are loyal and affectionate, and are much better suited to retired people than a young tearaway or a puppy. Few get the chance of a home, but with kindness and a little judicious dieting they can live for years.

If you choose a pedigree or a *known* crossbreed rather than a mutt (and I am a great fan of the mongrel), do find out about the breed. Pedigree traits are fairly predictable and it's no good adopting a cross-mastiff if you are eighty-five and live in a flat. There are rescue dogs to suit everyone's tastes, and if you can't find a soul-mate among them, then you're very hard to please.

Emma

Emma, or 'Splod', a Beardie cross, was the beloved friend of Annie Christie from Gosfield in Essex. 'I rescued Emma in 1993 – the family had no control over her. She became my little "right hand man" and everywhere I went Emma was sure to follow. She loved long walks alongside my mare Ria, and being in the car, staring avidly at the indicator level as if to say "Go on then – indicate – I know where we're going!" I love all my other doggies, but there will never be another Emma. We were soul-mates. I still miss her terribly.'

She practised being a person
All her days. Studying me
Finding out how to do it.
I laughed at her little traits
But she was a person
And she knew it.
Followed my feet, my fate
Running beside my horse
Swaying her shoulders
Cornering in the car
Knowing to indicate (of course)
And where the best walks are ...
Playing at hide and seek
Ready with infinite licks.
Lying across my lap
Having run out of tricks.

She never had a star.
She fixed on me
Her windblown person
Bringing up the rear
Following not from fear
But sheer delight.
Call her a dog if you like:
Nothing can quite erase
The light in her eager eyes
The oneness in all her ways.
These are the bonds that bind
Human and bird and beast.
No one was first or last.
Nothing that loves is least.

Jasmine

Police in Warwickshire broke into an abandoned garden shed and discovered a very frightened, starving female greyhound. She had obviously been abused. They took her to Nuneaton Warwickshire Wildlife Sanctuary (0247 634 5243), where she joined all the other lost and abandoned animals rescued by Geoff Grewcock and his team. 'Jasmine', as they called her, somehow felt she had been appointed to help run the place and welcome new waifs. She set about licking and mothering fox cubs, rabbits, pups, badger cubs, birds, chicks, guinea pigs and an eleven-week-old roe deer fawn. Years later beautiful Jasmine is still there, helping Geoff rescue the unwanted.

All the orphans, all the needy
All the battered and the broken
All the lost ones of Nuneaton
All are nuzzled on arrival:
All are welcomed at the shelter
Washed with lickings, washed with kisses
Washed and welcomed there by Jasmine
Patron Saint of the Unwanted.
Tiny pups, a pair of foundlings,
Tied on railway lines to die
Lifted by the scruff with whining
Placed so softly on the sofa
Jasmine settling, Jasmine nestling
Fox cubs, badger cubs and chickens
Nursing guinea pigs and rabbits
Letting birds perch on her long nose
(Jasmine could not hurt a fly).
Bramble, little roe deer baby
Found half-conscious in a meadow
Weak and wobbly, Jasmine mothered
Cuddling, covering with kindness
Trotting with him round the kennels
Eight legs mingling in their motion.
Did she learn to be so tender
From the sweetness of her owners?
No. We found her frightened, frail
Locked up and abused, abandoned.
Never judge books by their covers
Nor a dear dog by its tale.

4
BE PREPARED

Ex-shelter dogs may need a refresher course in housetraining. Battersea waifs used to go out with a message on their collars: 'Pray have a little patience with me. There are so many of us shut up together here that the keeper has no opportunity to teach us habits of cleanliness. I am quite willing to learn.'

Another difficulty for the adopted dog is a yen to trace its former owner, greatly missed. If you live close to their old haunts, you'll need to keep your adopted one on a lead or it will wander off. Give it time – it's a bit confused, that's all. The problem of wanderlust in general is much more common in males than in bitches. Males are assertive and adventurous and need firmer handling, so if you are submissive and shy yourself, you may be better off with a bitch. A male dog is rather like a poker player – he will examine you for your aces. Many police dogs have been reclaimed rejects and most are males, so you see what can be done, even with a large, potentially aggressive customer such as the German shepherd, by being firm, consistent and kind.

SEX, DRUGS AND ROCK AND ROLL

The answer to the question – 'dog or bitch?' – will also depend on which sexual habits you can put up with smilingly. Bitches have an oestrus or season twice a year, each lasting about three weeks. During this time they lose blood-stained fluid from the vagina and pester you to go out, hoping to be mated. They may, if thwarted, suffer a false pregnancy, start 'nesting' and be snappy if disturbed. They also attract local males who may congregate in your garden.

There are drugs and sprays to mask these problems, but they can be prevented once and for all by spaying. Males are not subject to 'heats' (unless they are racing dogs). Any time is right. If they sense a neighbourhood bitch in season, they become very frisky, wanting to get out. If frustrated, they may make a great escape bid, sulk, growl, mark their territory (urine stains the carpet) or make ludicrous attempts to mate with something in the house, such as a cushion or a visitor's leg. Again, such ardour can be controlled by drugs, but the vet may advise castration and if he does, please listen. Talk of neutering healthy animals may seem cruel, but consider the unwanted litter your pet may produce if he should escape – life isn't all that grand for them either, and at least your dog has a home. Vets and dog welfare workers recommend neutering because they see so many of the puppies. Of course, if you happen to have a gay dog like my late lamented mongrel Stanley, the problem doesn't arise. All that concerned *him* was the whereabouts of another mongrel called Sid.

APPEARANCE AND SIZE

Other choices such as coat-type and size are more straightforward. Long-haired luxury requires a lot of work if the coat isn't to become matted and may cause problems like runny eyes and embedded grass seeds. If you don't plan to groom your dog every day, either have it clipped or choose a smoothie. A smooth dog may moult in spring and summer, but a Mr Sheen in good condition is softer than mink and smoother than silk. A third type of coat, wiry or woolly, does not moult but needs professional clipping or stripping if you mean to keep it smart. Wiry and woolly dogs are hardy and have a certain Gaelic charm.

Size? This is really a matter of common sense. The bigger the dog, the more he will cost you to feed and the more mess he will make – of every sort – that you will have to clear up. I know of enormous dogs living happily in apartments, but they must have somewhere safe and free to run or they will feel cooped up and testy. If you fear burglars, a small dog's bark is just as effective a deterrent as a St Bernard's and consider *very* carefully before you adopt a big boisterous dog if you also have a child. The youngster won't be able to manage and there will be panic, a fight or a traffic accident. Larger dogs are very strong and can drag an adult after a cat or down the stairs.

You may weigh all the pros and cons, and then go to a shelter and come away with something completely different from what you intended. Many of us have. Don't worry about it. The dog you choose for its very awfulness will, given time, make itself beautiful in your eyes.

Lessa lives with her owners Keith and Margaret Miller and gorgeous Rough Collie Lass in the village of Ravenstone, Buckinghamshire. She came to England from Cyprus with Keith and Margaret after they successfully founded a huge modern dog rescue centre on the island, battling with politicians and bureaucrats and saving the lives of hundreds of dogs from cruelty and neglect. Lass and Daisy (another Rough Collie, who survived distemper) came over to join the Millers' English dogs Hestia, Aurora and Bacchus.

TEMPERAMENT

Appearance isn't everything, as every true dog lover knows. What about temperament? For some people, rescuing a dog becomes a pointless exercise unless they can save a lost soul as well – a dog who has been made completely miserable, hostile and scared by somebody else's cruelty. If you are such a person, no praise is too great, and there are enough moving testimonies in these pages from owners who have succeeded to make it worth a try. But please do it with your eyes open and don't, whatever you do, expect small children to help. Canine salvage is a delicate operation.

There are a few things you should know before you start. Firstly, most of the dogs who have ever savaged anyone have been male. Not all, but *most*. But any dog who is dominant, unpredictable, surly when reasonably chastised (*never* physically) and vengeful by nature is not to be trusted in your home. Secondly, there

Brandy came from the Danaher Rescue Centre at Wethersfield in Essex, which is independent but affiliated to the RSPCA. Diana Hulkes was looking for another dog after the loss of her beloved Willow as 'that had left a big hole both for me and my Labrador Bess'. Diana ended up choosing something completely different from what she intended. It was meant to be! 'Four years old when I had her, Brandy is six now, and you couldn't wish for a better companion.'

are very few mad mongrels, since they have not been subjected to close breeding or purpose-breeding for aggression like certain pure-breds that are known to throw volatile strains. Most behaviour problems in mongrels are not due to inherent nuttiness but to bad habits ingrained by mismanagement. Thirdly, if you take on any dog with these habits, you may be inheriting problems that led to the previous eviction of this dog, and aggression, dirtiness and noisiness are the most common. These habits are by no means impossible to eradicate, but they will take time and patience. Forewarned is forearmed. Lastly, you must not wallop the dog if he gets it wrong, or he will go backwards not forwards.

SENSIBLE PRECAUTIONS

Ask the shelter staff for details of your new dog's diet and stick to what it has been used to at first – this will avoid unduly upsetting a worried tummy. Collect the dog in the morning if you possibly can – that way it will have time to get used to your house before darkness falls and it has to sleep in a strange bed. Don't make a detour from the kennels to show your new pet to friends: come straight home. For a rescue dog the journey may be hair-raising. Have someone with you if you can, to comfort the dog as you go along.

Have everything ready at home before you arrive – its water and food bowls, its bed or box or rug, and lots of newspaper for toilet training. Have the garden fixed up: it's no good mending the fences after your bounder has bolted. Protect your pond and your prize bulbs – don't wait for the newcomer to dig them up and then give it a hiding.

And finally, please *don't* bring your rescue dog home as a Christmas present. Noisy festive seasons are not the time to be housetraining a frightened orphan. Remember, 'A dog is for life…'

'FEELING WITH'

Whatever rescue dog you choose, and wherever you get it from, life will be a lot easier if, at the outset, *you put yourself in the dog's place*. I know a lot of people will say this book is full of anthropomorphism, and dogs are not human and 'don't have feelings like us'. Well, actually they do, and growing scientific evidence is emerging from studies of animal emotions. Empathy with a dog companion is not some trifling fantasy invented by sad and lonely owners. Empathy is 'feeling with'. Compassion is 'feeling with'. Sympathy is 'feeling with'. We owe it to companion animals to try to understand them. That's what the poems are all about. Once you see a dog as an individual with feelings, with signs and signals and expressions, you will begin to interpret them correctly, and you will therefore train and communicate with the dog correctly, and your reward will be abounding love and joy.

Otto

Otto the Lurcher started life as 'Munchie'. He and his sister Pickles were stolen as puppies from Dogs Trust Evesham Rehoming Centre in October 2009. Five months on and 171 miles away in Kent, a lone emaciated pup was found running round a hospital car park. Identified from his microchip, Munchie was taken to Dogs Trust Canterbury where he caught the eye of Tessa and Stuart Wheeler, owners of Chilham Castle. Says Tessa: 'I found myself instantly taken by Munchie.' Now known as 'Otto', he presides over 320 acres and hopes soon to be 'mingling' on their garden open days.

Stolen in the dead of night:
Caught with Pickles by the scruff.
Shoved in cages out of sight
And driven off.
Rough men speeding us away
Taking us we knew not where.
Pickles nuzzles me to say
'Evesham's back there!'
Bundled out in some strange land.
Waited till their guard was down.
Wrestled from a filthy hand
And ran to town.
'Someone help me – I've come far!
I'm a pup, and desperate!'
Warden took me in his car
And to the vet.
Rubbed me with a Meter Peeper.
Found the chip that said my name.
Called the Dogs Trust as my keeper.
Dogs Trust came!
Happy ending to my story.
Lady saw me hang my head
Missing little Pickles sorely.
'You shall live in style,' she said.
Now I am her castle keeper,
Grounds as far as I can spy.
All this from a chip and Peeper.
(This is not a porkie pie.)

Zak

Zak the Collie lived with the Burder family at their homes in Shimpling and Long Melford, Suffolk, where many Border Collies have been treasured over the years. Originally from Wales he became John Burder's favourite dog, and when John passed away Zak looked after widowed Dorothy ('Dot') and their son David. Zak loved games of fetch and squeaked his toys tirelessly, being very clever at obedience and agility work. He died of cancer but was a most brave boy – always cheerful and willing to obey. Sadly missed.

Zak's a good boy now. No sheep?
I'll round up your chickens. Or your ducks.
How can I please you? I know, I'll do this:
Squeak squeak with my toy
In time to the music. Look, I can do this:
Zigzag, weaving through the sticks
On the obstacle course, racing to retrieve
Two things in my mouth, or three
No matter to me, so long as I can please you.
Master I loved. I was under his feet
In every shed with my Dad.
And when he went to the sky
I kept my eager eye on Mistress for my cues.
Their son, I wait by his hand to run.
Born in Bala, brought up in a storm
I was a bad pup, nipped with needle teeth.
Ashamed, I deserved to lose my home.
They took me to the shelter in a storm again.
So many storms for a young pup to bear.
And I languished there. All the other dogs
Were treasured up and taken but not me.
Nobody wants a biter. So
I bowed my head really low
And let my life away, and didn't care all day.
But then out of despair my people came
And picked me out, and said my name.
Which is why I long to please them.
Bad leg? Ill? Doesn't matter to me
Running through the cloth sausage
Wanting to fetch for Mistress,
Wanting to be brave in the storm
And do no harm. A dog can reform.
A dog can learn. A dog can be reborn.
Zak's a good boy now.

5

HOME FROM HOME:

TRAINING

A TRIP TO A shelter, you may think, must be terribly depressing. Not if you intend to take a dog home. It is like being at large in a jeweller's silly sale.

The kennel staff will often know quite a bit about a dog's temperament, though some cast-offs don't take to being kennelled and behave badly because they are institutionalised. There are noisy barkers, for example, and dogs that will nip a neighbouring tail when it pokes through their netting, who when they get to the right sort of home can be restored to perfectly normal pets. Most can be rehabilitated to some extent.

Many inmates have been thrown out at the peak eviction time of around six months to a year, when pretty puppyhood ends and teething and lack of training begin to cause inconvenience. These are the doggie delinquents – no idea of discipline but leaping with enthusiasm: 'young idiots', as one rescue manager put it, 'who've been allowed to run riot'. Some of the larger charities spay all bitches old enough to have a season and castrate males on veterinary advice, although it takes six months for the hormones to change. Males may be neutered for aggression, wandering and leaping the fence. It makes the dogs more like homebodies.

GIVING THEM TIME

All rescue dogs desperately need one thing: *an owner who can give them time.* Dogs are social people. They can all learn, and as you can see from so many of our verses, they can reform. Imagine a zigzag that starts wide at one end and gradually tapers down to a simple line. This is the pattern of rehabilitation. You start with wild 'zigs' and 'zags' and gradually these swings and excesses calm down to a wavy line, steady and straight with an occasional wiggle.

Some of the rescue centres have an information sheet on each kennel, offering prospective adopters all the news they have about the waif within. One of the details given is invariably 'Reason for Re-homing', and often this box will contain three terrible words that may doom a dog: 'COULD NOT COPE'. *Please cope.*

TRAIN OR BE TRAINED

A word of advice before we get down to the nitty-gritty of homebody training. If you do not train your dog, your dog will train you. Rescue dogs are in a very high league mentally, and crossbreeds and mongrels in particular are born survivors. This means they are in a good position to do as they think fit, if you allow them to. They have strong views on doggie government and how they wish to conduct their affairs – a mentality often born of hardship. So if you bring one home, be it an adult or a puppy, you should expect to spend some time showing it the house rules. Set the tone of your relationship from the very start. If you do not assume authority, you will leave a vacuum that your rescue dog will quickly fill, particularly a male dog, accustomed to competing for all his wants.

The traditional theory of dog training or 'breaking' (note the expression) has always been based on dominance: the concept that you impose yourself on the dog as his new pack leader, to be feared and obeyed. The 'show it who's boss' philosophy has given rise to a great deal of cruelty, sticks, switches, electric shock collars, spiked chains and choke chains to physically coerce the dog into obedience.

It is perfectly possible to have authority over a dog without cruelty, and if you are dealing with an adult animal from a shelter, you have a particular responsibility to avoid brutal coercion, not only on ethical grounds but because brutal methods may force the dog into a corner from which its only recourse is savage revenge. Wolves, which sort out their internal status feuds on the alpha dominance principle, may be awfully wild and grand, but they also have horrific and fatal fights. If this is the basis on which you wish to train your dog, one or both of you may end up very badly injured. Dogs have forty-two teeth, humans thirty-two. It's up to you.

SENIOR PARTNER

The other way of training a dog is to act as senior partner, based on the principle that you know more than he does. This method is based on three rules: be firm, be fair and be kind. Put yourself in the dog's place and try to simplify things for him (or her – I use the masculine only for convenience). Remember, he's just a dog. He's not as clever as you. He may be more in tune with nature and more able with his nose and ears, but his vocabulary is very limited. Don't talk to him as if he is a member of Mensa. He won't get you. You may have to go over something repeatedly before your dog sees what you have in mind.

Be consistent – don't reward him for some momentarily amusing behaviour one minute and punish him for it the next. Be patient. A dog's greatest happiness is to be best pals with his owner and he desperately wants to live with you and not be turned out and abandoned again. Praise will always be remembered better than scolding because the latter is painful to recall. So try to engineer the dog into a position where you can praise him for something if you can, rather than moaning at him all the time. Never, ever, lose your temper. Remember these are damaged goods.

Jayne Stevenson and her husband from Olney, Bucks, rescue down-and-out dogs. Says Jayne: 'Stan was in a terrible state. He'd been found wandering in East Wick, Olney, and we had him registered with Milton Keynes police as a serious neglect case. Stan could hardly walk. I put my hand out by way of greeting and he sniffed my hand, and that was it. I said "He's coming with us". His vet bills cost hundreds of pounds, so I wrote an article in Phonebox and kind readers made donations, and sent bedding. Stan had lots of fans. He became very popular, plodding about the market with me. We had him less than a year before he died, but he did have that happiness.'

The easiest way is to return to basics. If you bring home an adult dog with some ingrained bad habit, try to work out the reason for his behaviour – what he fears and what he gains by it. Use your insight. A dog is an animal without any moral compass. He only learns what he may or may not do by your responses. These can be very puzzling. He may have been inadvertently 'rewarded' for doing what you don't want him to do. Without necessarily realising it, previous owners may have been flattered by him fearlessly protecting them and barking furiously at strangers or showing jealousy towards another family member who sits near them on the sofa. The dog may have drawn the wrong conclusions about what is required to keep humans happy. He cannot grasp threats of future reprisals, or wrongdoings of this morning being punished this afternoon. Simplify, and you will see the situation from the dog's point of view.

ASSUMING AUTHORITY

Some people have natural authority over a dog. Most do not. If you don't have this natural charisma you will have to assume it, and this will not be achieved by ranting and raving or waving your arms in the air. When crises occur, as they sometimes do, drop your voice an octave, slow down and be prepared to repeat yourself. Keep control. Keep your back straight and your arms at your sides so you present a solid shape. The late great Sir

Laurence Olivier once observed that an audience respects an actor who never has to fully extend himself. Dogs know by your delivery whether you're about to bust a gasket or be master of the situation.

You are the leader of this dog. You go through the door first, not him. You go through gates and entrances first. You have your dinner first (and have a 'pretend' taste of bits of his before he is served his dish). When you come home, *ignore him.* Calmly take your coat off and go and put your things down or your shopping in the kitchen. *Then* greet the dog and make a fuss of him. This has to be the order of events in your home, because he must understand that this is your house and you are in charge of all comings and goings – not him. A rescue dog is often an *insecure* dog. Give him the stability of knowing there's somebody in charge here who will look after things and keep order. The dog then doesn't have to take charge, and in fact most don't *want* that huge burden of responsibility anyway.

Try to avoid head-to-head confrontations, big 'scenes' and battles of will. A dog can be easily diverted from a bad pattern of behaviour at the outset by simple planned tactics. One of the best diversion strategies I've seen was demonstrated to me by the country's leading authority on problem dogs, Dr Roger Mugford. This involves the use of an old coat or towel thrown on the floor, a rape alarm and a few nourishing titbits. The dog must be on the lead. At the outset of a dotty turn, the rape alarm is set off, the dog is led briskly on its lead to sit on the coat or towel and a titbit is given, followed by much praise. I've seen the method employed in Dr Mugford's surgery to great effect on biters, barkers and delinquents. A few such exercises can baffle a dog into submission and reform even the most entrenched bad habits by substituting a new pattern of behaviour.

Timmy – very young, wiry, glossy and extremely scarred – is the most recent addition to the Hilling household in Essex. The first night he spent in his happy new home he slept not a wink in case it was all too good to be true. The second night tiredness finally got the better of him. Timmy is now a whirlwind of activity, having thrown Cindy to the ground through sheer exuberance once or twice. She says: 'Timmy is a very active fun-loving greyhound. He has had a lot of problems in his life but tries hard to overcome them.'

Another very useful tip on the initial homecoming of a known 'problem' dog (and by no means all rescue dogs have these issues) comes from kennel managers at the shelters, who say the best way to rehabilitate the beastie is to keep it with you constantly, never letting it out of your sight or scent but at the same time *ignoring* it and going about your business quite normally. Let the dog see your routines and that you do not intend to harm or smother him, and he will come to you when he is ready. Only a tiny percentage of problem dogs fail to respond when they find themselves safe and sound.

Bracken

I'm Bracken, I'm barmy.
They all try to calm me.
I'm bonkers, I'm up in your face.
I'm a climber, a jumper,
A bouncer, a bumper
With one ear all over the place.

I'm a Lurcher, a barger,
A writher, a charger,
I'm not like these greyhounds you see.
I'm a bounder, I'm bolder,
One leg on your shoulder –
Oh don't look at them – look at me!

They took me for training
But I'd be there straining:
I like to live life to the max!
I know why they dump us –
For riot and rumpus.
I'm Bracken, and these are the facts.

Bonnie

The Maltese Dog

Little Bonnie was the guardian of author and *Daily Mail* advice columnist Bel Mooney. Bonnie was found abandoned, tied to a tree in Bath. She was tiny but fearless and, as explained in Bel's moving autobiographical *Small Dogs Can Save Your Life*, helped her owner survive the break-up of her first marriage. Bonnie resembled the faithful lapdog of Mary Queen of Scots, found under her skirts after her beheading at Fotheringhay Castle, and this is why the sonnet form seemed right for her.

When I am dark she doth all brightness make
Her jewel eyes outwitting my great cares
Beckoning me with quivers and with stares
To join her in her world and in her wake.
Business she shows me, precious truth and sense
(Urgent she moves for time is short as limbs):
Leaves she must toss and earth with wonders brims
That she must scent and snuff with needs intense.
Careless of self, this little stranger came
To guard me, fierce and faithful, while I sleep
Giving her fragile strength, her passions deep
A mighty being in a tiny frame.
Who dares call her a cast-off and a toy
Knows not such vibrant and redeeming joy.

Bess

Bess's owners are Penny and John Avant. They spotted her at Exeter RSPCA, where she had given up barking and was about to give up altogether. They brought her home and she was eager to learn 'so long as treats were involved'. Says Penny: 'We were told she was between four and five years old. Bess is a wonderful companion, smiling first thing in the morning and sitting on our feet whenever possible.' Her new hobbies are running in circles (to acclaim), playing fetch and leaping waves on the beach.

I was called Bolts and my sister was Nails.
Bad naughty Bolts! they said, bad naughty Nails!
We'd go hell for leather, rip roaring together
and flinging ourselves in a flailing fierce
Furfight flat out for cats' tails.
Off to the RSPCA with you, those owners said.
Somebody took us though, somebody brave ...
Skirmishes over looks, scrummages over smells
We'd still knock seven bells
out of each other and couldn't behave.
Back to the RSPCA. So I said to Nails
It's your blasted fault – now we're banged up all day.
But Nails could do languid looks. Poor little soul they said
Petting and patting her head like a pup.
So Nails gets picked up! Well, I stood and stared.
Never a bark was heard. Never a tear was shed.
What about me? I said – nobody cared. So then I got scared.
Good job this couple came tossing a ball.
Now that's what I call
A top game for dogs of ability, dogs of agility
Dogs of nobility like me to play. I was in thrall!
Suddenly I had a hearth and a home
And a seaside to roam and two cuddlers to lick,
Woods and long walkies and games with a stick.
They don't say 'naughty Bolts'. Now I'm 'sweet Bess'.
What a good time I get now I'm these people's pet:
Living the high life – that's girl power I guess.

6
WHAT YOU WILL NEED

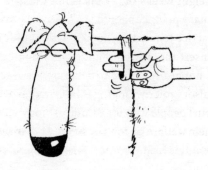

WALKIES

Your rescue dog has struck it lucky. Hundreds of thousands don't. Yours will not rake the streets or be shut in a shed, tied up, chained up or locked in a garage. Yours will be a homebody, with a collar and lead and proper walks and a bed to go to when life gets on top of him. A collar and lead are your dog's first steps to civilisation. A rolled leather or flat collar with a metal nameplate that can be engraved with your phone number is ideal. If there's no nameplate, you can attach an identity disc by the key-ring principle, though these sometimes get lost.

Under new legislation you must now have your pet microchipped, and this has long been recommended by some of the major charities. Read the verse story of young Otto, who might never have ended up living in a magnificent castle, or indeed anywhere *at all*, had it not been for his Dogs Trust microchip.

From April 2016 the Microchipping of Dogs (England) Regulations 2014 have been enforced by local authorities, the police and other government-appointed bodies. Under the law all dogs must now be registered to an approved database by the time they are eight weeks old. This is not difficult to arrange and any veterinary practice should be able to help you. The cost varies from practice to practice, but it takes only a few moments to painlessly insert the tiny chip under your dog's skin, and he or she should hopefully be identifiable on recovery if lost or stolen. Compulsory microchipping is intended to bear down on ruthless and cruel people who breed and sell dogs without proper concern for their welfare or for any harm or damage they may cause. A collar and identification are also required by law when your dog goes out.

The more identification your dog has, the better. In the last two years, dog thefts have soared by 20 per cent. Targeted in particular are the new fashionable breeds and crossbreeds, and pets favoured by celebrities. 'On trend' are Pugs and little French Bulldogs and any tiny 'toy' breeds – like those carried about in the arms or handbags of actresses and pop stars – that can be snatched from cars or gardens. Those who regard dogs as commodities see a way to make money out of misery. Between January 2013 and April 2016, 5,288 dogs were reported stolen and each year the numbers soar. In 2013, 1,490 dogs were stolen, 1,599 in 2014, 1,776 in 2015, rising to 423 in the first three months of 2016 alone. There is also a growing problem with dog theft for ransom, preying on the owner's love for the dog and looking to gain a reward for its return.

Watch your dog. Don't leave it exposed alone in your garden or tied outside a shop where it may be targeted by dog-snatchers. Consider purchasing one of the numerous sat-tracking collar devices that can locate your pet if it goes missing. Wherever possible, take your dog with you, and never, ever leave it in a hot car. Even with the windows slightly open, temperatures can soar in under ten minutes and literally roast your friend to death. Every summer many dogs have to be rescued from boiling metal cells, and for some, help comes too late. Try to work out a sensible balance between travelling about with your dog and leaving it at home; between keeping your dog safe but giving it a decent, stimulating life. After all, it is highly intelligent and needs to see the world just as you do.

One of the best ways of ensuring your friend has a varied, interesting life is to give it at least two or three walks a day. Please don't let it be one of nearly half a million imprisoned dogs in the country that are never exercised outside their homes or gardens. Walking is exceptionally good for you, both physically and mentally. It keeps you fit and agile and lifts depression – a win-win situation. There is also a great social side. You meet other dog owners and quickly get to know the characters on either end of the lead; indeed, I've made some very good friends that way.

The lead should be of strong bridle leather or nylon, 1–2.5 metres long depending on your height, with a bolt-action trigger hook to attach to the collar. The lead should be slack as you walk. Collars are too tight if you can't get two fingers under them when they are done up, and too loose if the dog can jerk his head out and get away. For a very small adult without much pulling power, a harness may be better. Some little dogs suffer from windpipe problems that can be aggravated by a collar.

You may also consider some training equipment to make your life easier. A Flexi-lead, which works rather like an angler's winch, unreeling and locking, or a training lead of nylon cord, 9–14 metres long with a hook collar clasp at the end, can be bought from any decent pet shop and will give you control even at a distance while your dog is learning the ropes. You could, if all else fails, attach a hook clasp to a washing line in the garden for training sessions. A little pup will need an interim 'baby' collar and lead; don't spend a lot on this as it will be quickly outgrown.

CHOKE CHAINS

Many trainers recommend the choke chain which they call, euphemistically, a 'check' chain. It works by choking the dog when it pulls and, if worn the wrong way round, can be catastrophic. Injudicious use of choke chains has caused serious injuries: neuromuscular disorders from constriction of the cervical region of the spine, ruptured windpipes, bruising to the outer and inner ears and epileptic fits triggered by constriction of the blood supply to the brain. Animal behaviourist Dr Roger Mugford researched these injuries and came up with an alternative – called the Halti – that is now widely available. See www. companyofanimals.co.uk. It consists of a simple web of straps that fits over the dog's face. It stops him from pulling by controlling his head – as a halter controls a horse. The packaging tells you how to put it on and how to get the dog used to it (there may be initial objections to the strangeness).

Unlike cat-owners, who in the UK may legally allow their pets to use public places and other people's gardens as toilets, dog owners are required by law to clear up mess. Both dogs and cats can transmit diseases harmful to human health (zoonoses) and there is a great deal of misunderstanding about the relative dangers involved with the two species. Stringent laws on dog 'fouling' were introduced because of an extremely rare disease, ocular toxocariasis, which in some vulnerable children can cause blindness. The disease with symptoms is so rare that most doctors have never even seen a case and children affected often suffer from coprophagia or soil-eating. This unusual disease is caused by the toxocara parasite transmitted to the soil in dog and cat faeces. In the dog the nematode is called toxocara canis, and in the cat toxocara cati. In studies around the world most cat populations have been found to carry the parasite. Cats can also transmit several other diseases highly dangerous to humans, including helicobacter pylori, TB and the potentially deadly toxoplasmosis.

It is strange, then, that dog 'fouling' has attracted swingeing fines while cat 'littering' is regarded as harmless. Dogs have been banned from many public areas, pubs, parks and beaches for health and safety reasons, and these dog bans are spreading throughout the country. So I suggest dog owners do three things. Firstly, be responsible and carry a couple of plastic bags to clear up when you take your dog for a walk to avoid public hysteria. Secondly, form local dog owners' groups to represent your interests. And thirdly, write to your MP about any canophobic injustice you may perceive. Dog owners pay 20 per cent VAT on all pet food and products, veterinary treatment and even euthanasia. No taxation without representation.

INSURANCE

Veterinary treatment is an unavoidable expense for any dog owner, and you need to understand that health costs have recently skyrocketed, partly because animal medicine is not VAT exempt.

Many dogs currently languishing in rescue centres are there because their owners could not or would not afford veterinary treatment. The PDSA (People's Dispensary for Sick Animals), Blue Cross and RSPCA clinics rely on donations and have therefore to be judicious about which hard-up pet-owners they can help. You are strongly urged to get your dog insured, and some charities, like the Greyhound Trust, provide interim insurance as part of the asking price of your new dog. There are dozens of pet insurance schemes on the market so shop around. Many policies include third-party cover to protect you from liability for any damage or accident caused by your dog during its lifetime.

PREPARING YOUR HOME

What else will you need? Most vets and trainers would say an enclosed garden, please. It is possible to housetrain a dog in a flat, but it requires a lot of patience and ingenuity, use of a litter tray early on, followed by much running up and down stairs with your pet on a lead, sometimes in your dressing gown.

Penny came from Romford Greyhound Owners and is one of the Hilling troupe of rescue greyhounds on the borders of Essex and Suffolk. She invariably looks worried, as she has a lot of parenting problems. Cindy Hilling: 'She is a real mum to her dozens of furry toys and is usually to be found with one of her "babies" in her mouth. She once woke us up at three in the morning in order to rescue a baby she had left outside.'

A garden makes all your training work so much simpler. Fences must be secure; if there is a hole in the hedge, your dog will find it.

Fence off any part of the garden where the newcomer must not go and cover fish ponds with wire netting. Check to see that gates shut properly and that an amorous hound can't squeeze underneath. Unfortunately, dogs can also dig and jump. A Boxer or German Shepherd can scale a seven-foot fence and Terriers are champion burrowers. Survey your garden carefully until you know the measure of your dog's capabilities. And please don't ever go out and leave a dog chained to a fence or post. It is very cruel.

Indoors you will need a couple of dog bowls – earthenware ones are ideal for water as they don't tip all over the floor. If you have a tall dog, bowls may be raised up by placing them on a secure stand or on suitably sized plastic bins. The water bowl must always be available *where your dog can reach it*. The second bowl is for food – better than a plate because doggie noses push food over the edge and make a mess. Wash both regularly and thoroughly. A safe dog-chewable toy, such as a *big* cowhide bone, will provide a useful distraction from the furniture, but best not to allow unsupervised hide-chewing: 'Kong' toys (ask at the pet shop) can be stuffed with food that will take the dog a good while to get at.

DIET

I strongly recommend that you stick to the food that your dog has been given at the shelter, at least initially, as sudden changes in diet can play havoc with dogs' tums. After that you can choose from the vast variety of dog diets out there, but please read the labels and follow the feeding guidelines for your dog's weight. If you choose dry food, either soak it in gravy or provide water beside the bowl (*you* try swallowing a lot of un-moistened kibble and see how you like it). Ideally feed the dog a moist food with a mixer, so he gets the best of both worlds. The packaging will give instructions on the correct proportions. Always consider paying a little extra for natural ingredients, rather than settling for animal derivatives off the abattoir floor. Finally, your own mealtime leftovers are *not* an appropriate diet for your dog. Some human foods can give him dandruff and nutrient deficiencies. Some can make him enormously fat. And some, like onions, raisins, grapes or chocolate, can actually poison him.

BEDTIME

Finally, your dog will need a bed. For a little needle-toothed pup, always chewing, a cardboard box with an entrance cut out of one side and an old blanket or sweater is quite adequate. For an adult, pet shops and suppliers offer a huge range of options from rigid plastic ones that you can line with blankets and scrub out to fibreglass ones with gentle warming panels in the base, to soft and luxurious stuffed beds and bean-beds (for the dog that can keep his teeth to himself), and expensive orthopaedic beds that make older, creakier dogs comfy. For a giant breed you could even use a folded single duvet that you can periodically stick in the washing machine.

Whichever you choose, place the bed in a corner away from draughts and paddling feet. This will be your dog's refuge, and please allow him privacy in it – all dogs sleep during part of the day. The bed of an adult should be big enough for him to turn round and round in before he settles.

Bringing your rescue dog home, you will probably find that bedtime is the hardest part of the day. When you turn out the light and retire, having praised the creature in its bed, there will be a short silence followed by whimpering and whining, and possibly even barking. Go downstairs and say *No!* very firmly. If it persists you can either repeat the procedure or take the dog and dog-bed to your room for a night or two, particularly if this is a puppy. When the house is no longer weird and frightening, you should find your orphan will sleep anywhere in it, and not mind at all.

Outside kennels are not to be recommended for a companion animal intended to share your life, and some dogs' homes specifically ask you to keep their adoptees indoors. If a dog is not good enough to live in your house, perhaps it is not good enough for you altogether, and a lot of dogs from shelters have spent quite enough time stuck out in all weathers, thank you very much.

Ouzo

Rob and Helen Simpson were on holiday on the Greek island of Zakynthos when they spotted Ouzo roaming the streets. She would beg for sausages and chicken. Says Helen Simpson: 'When we got home we went on the internet and discovered Zakynthos Dog Rescue. Two very kind English ex-pat ladies helped us get Ouzo rounded up. Sadly when they got her into the van her doggie friend tried to follow, but they couldn't take him.' Ouzo now lives in Long Melford, Suffolk. When she smells sausages and chicken cooking she jumps for joy.

Tiger and Tilly

Tiger is fourteen and Tilly is twelve. They have lived with Claire Hannan for seven years since she spotted them at the RSPCA Wethersfield shelter in Essex. The two were about to be split up as nobody wanted the pair, but this would have broken their spirits. The lovers are inseparable. Tiger barks with fury at all comers if he is out with Tilly, and 'if you try to take Tiger out without Tilly she will hurl herself at the door to be with him'. They sleep together wrapped in Claire's duvet, play together and eat together, including the bag of seed.

Waste not want not
Thought Tiger and Tilly, tucking in
To the bag of birdseed on the floor.
Their owner found them grainy-nosed
And asked them sternly who did what.
'That Tilly started it', thought Tiger
Which was an utter lie.
His ball-of-fire behaviour
Meant they couldn't go far
Or travel anywhere in the car
Due to his lathered barking
At passing dogs and passers-by.
It brought shame on them both,
Poor Tilly thought
For she was dainty in her ways.
But she was Tiger's pride and all his stars:

Tilly being from Venus

And Tiger being from Mars.

Sidney

Sidney McGee was the beloved gentle pal of the author when she lived in London. But he had not been home a week before her mother was pleading for him to go back whence he came (Wood Green Animal Shelter, Heydon). Despite problems with destruction while he was settling in, Sid turned out to have an angelic temperament and became known to all as 'Doglet'. In old age he developed a plump sailor's roll. A small boy, noticing this waddle, observed: 'Look Dad – that dog's going side by side.'

A problem dog is someone who
After you've terribly kindly come
To rescue him and take him home
Leaps through the window of your car
And runs back in the shelter door;
Then, setting off for somewhere remote
Stands up behind, forelegs in play
And grasping them round the driver's throat
Throttles you on the motorway.
A problem dog is one who chews
Whenever you go out, and drags
Your carpet up against the door
Dismembering his toys, your shoes
And, most dramatically of all,
The sofa seats, leaving the bags.
A problem dog is one who grows
Steadily safe when left alone –
You will be back, this is his home –
Who puts behind him former woes,
And wags and welcomes you instead,
So even those who thought him bad
Grudgingly praise and pat his head.
A problem dog is one who steals
Your heart at last when it's too late:
When he is precious, old and grey
And loudly you lament his fate.
Treasure your problem dog because
One day it's certain, he'll leave you
Bereft and scared as he once was
With nothing suitable to chew.

7
THE FIRST DAY

ON'T EXPECT TOO much; keep the proceedings low key. Show your newcomer his bed and bowls. Don't be surprised if there is no appetite at homecoming. Canine stomachs are queasy in a crisis and this is a crisis, for your rescue dog if not for you. He thinks: 'Oh no, I've been farmed out to some more people now, and these will get rid of me tomorrow. Nobody wants a poor cast-off dog.'

Be kind and gentle. Take several opportunities to say what a good dog he is. Imagine how you'd feel. Try to resist bunging a dogs-home waif into a bath of hot water or hosing him down in the garden on the very first day, unless you have brought home a very amenable personality. Let the shockwaves roll over him rather gradually. Show him the garden and say, 'Look what you've got!' As you can see from some of our versified stories, he may never have seen grass or flowers before, let alone a tree. Memories of past thrashings will begin to fade. You may even discern a little wag struggling to express itself, though wags may be slow in coming.

Please try to ensure that you're about the house all day on this special occasion, and avoid distressing the newcomer further by leaving him alone. Think of this as your new dog's birthday and take the day off work! Introduce the family without tumult or fuss, and be sure to let the orphan sleep as much as he wants. Sleep knits up the ravelled sleeve of care.

A NAME

Choose a name for your dog and stick to it, because this is a key word for your pet to learn. If he or she arrives with a name from the shelter that you can't stand, try to adapt it to something similar to avoid confusion. You don't have to call your dog Fido or Sandy. Use your imagination. What about Wallace, Holly, Noah, Joss, Kate, Poppy, Tuffy, Dinsdale, Hattie, Ralph, Maud, Bosie, Butler, Madge, Blondie, Oswald, Peg, Baxter, Dingo, Sidney, Sunny, Mo, Stanley, Geoffrey, Star, Chip, Pip, Oliver, Albert, Flower, Johnson, Moll, Harriet, or Daisy Dumpling?

TOILET TRAINING

You should begin toilet training on Day One. Pups are little orphans – orphan wetting and orphan messing. They sleep a lot and have frequent meals, and a puppy under three months has no more control over rear-end mysteries than a human baby. When it wakes up and after meals, or when it shows signs of wanting to relieve itself (urgent scratching, circling or squatting), pick the pup up, put it down gently in the garden and when it wets or defecates say 'Garden!' and praise it lavishly. It will then associate the word 'garden' with the toilet, and with much patience you can trigger the bodily function by using the sound, in the same way that Pavlov caused dogs to salivate to the sound of bells and tuning forks. 'Garden' is where your dog's natural functions will cause the least offence to the fastidious British public.

Indoors at night you will need some newspaper. A pup will not usually soil his own bed and will prefer newspaper to a cold floor. Over a period of time, move the newspaper zone nearer and nearer the back door until finally, as the puppy watches, you place it just outside. This will make the 'Garden' transition easier for it to understand, and eventually you'll find the creature at the back door when nature calls. Do let it out promptly, even if you're busy, or you may have to go back to square one. There may be errors. Clean them up with a little disinfectant and spray the spot with a deodoriser.

Housetraining may take several weeks. Scold the dog when it makes a mistake, putting it immediately in the garden, but never rub its nose in the puddle. To an animal with such highly developed scenting equipment this is very cruel. If you catch the miscreant in the very act, noise is the best rebuff. Slap a newspaper in your hand or bang an old tin tray. Don't punish the dog for an 'old' puddle. He has no knowledge of history and will think he is being scolded for his present behaviour – which may be greeting you when you come home. Remember, dogs learn by association, not 'morals'.

A dogs' home adult waif that has not been housetrained at all is less common than one that has lapsed through being shut in kennels. In any case, you should use exactly the same methods as for a pup and persevere: 'Garden' first thing in the morning, last thing at night and after meals. Lavish praise when it does its stuff, repeating the word 'garden' till it sounds to you like gobbledegook. Have patience: don't lecture the dog, and don't blame him for incompetence. One sound, however monotonous to you, is easier for him to remember: the Guide Dog Association use the word 'busy'.

An adult rescue dog may have no idea of bowel or bladder control. He may take a long time to get his degree in potty science, just like a puppy, and an adult male's problem is

> Willow the Shepherd Cross was discovered at Willow Tree Sanctuary in Gainsford End, Essex, and taken to live on a farm in Gosfield by Diana Hulkes. Her dam was 'a little yellow crossbreed' and her sire a very handsome German Shepherd, both inmates at the shelter. Says Diana: 'Dear Willow – a guard till the end. At nine and a half a bit portly, but always game, always ready for a walk and always trusted her vet.'

compounded by the fact that he cocks his leg against the vertical to trigger urination, which if he is shut indoors means one of your walls or a piece of furniture. If you have particular problems like this the vet may be able to help, as there are drugs to suppress male hormone marking in the house. Otherwise try the simple expedient of putting the dog's bed in a room with a tiled or linoleum surface and newspaper, as for puppies, and restricting the area at night by means of a 'pen'. Feed the dog at regular times and it will generally defecate at regular times. Avoid feeding him late at night. Flat-dwellers with either a pup or an adult will need a cat-litter tray, again moved gradually nearer the door.

SPRAYING

There is another sort of toilet problem – spraying. Some dogs and some bitches 'spray' when they are very excited, such as when they are thrilled you have come home. Don't smack the dog – it can't help it, and it may have been trying to control itself with a full bladder. Take it into the garden for now, and consult your veterinary surgeon.

Finally, when you are walking your dog in public places, remember to clear up after him with a plastic bag and dispose of it in a bin. Please don't risk that fine and disgrace the rest of us. We have enough trouble with bans as it is.

Tim

Tim was saved from a place in Suffolk by a volunteer with the Labrador Lifeline Trust, John Westgate. He is adored by his new Norfolk family and their Cocker Spaniel Winnie, from whom he is inseparable. He has made a complete recovery from his cold life and frostbitten ears. Says the charity's Anne Carter: 'Each day he seems to take another step forward. It is only through the love and kindness shown by his adopted family that this little dog now lives a normal and happy life.'

Oliver

Oliver was born in Cyprus, and was rescued from his miserable existence by an Englishwoman and brought back to Britain. Sadly the lady fell ill and died and her family decided to move to America, so poor Ollie was homeless once again. That was until he met Mrs Audrey Crawley of Halstead in Essex – it was love at first sight. Daughter Marian finds Ollie can sometimes be 'a monkey' about going for walkies or getting in the car, but Audrey couldn't wish for better: 'He is an excellent, loyal and brilliant housedog and companion.'

Ollie is flowing in the wind.
His ears, as he sits in the car,
Ripple gently like the hair
Of an actress in an old film noir.
Ollie has lost some teeth.
His grin is a little sucked in,
The hairy chin beneath.

Ollie adores his Mum
Such that, when she comes home,
He throws back his head and howls:
Howls from his deepest tum.

Except when she returned
From the Hip Op.
Would not greet.
Would not speak.
Sat with his back to her for a week.

Ollie the obstinate boy
Cannot be bustled when late.
If he wants to sit, he'll sit.
If he wants to go back, that's it.

Oliver, proud as a prince.
Third home lucky, happy ever since
(Apart from the business of the Op
Which did necessitate a strop.)

Peek

The Dogs Trust in Basildon gave us the following information about yellow Lab Peek. 'He is an older dog (8+) but still very active and a fast learner. He is at his happiest being kept busy and mentally stimulated or going for long walks to burn off some energy. Peek is a curious boy looking to eat his way into someone's life as he loves his food and will happily work for treats. He is very friendly to both dogs and strangers and loves a fuss and to be the centre of attention. Peek loves a game of fetch and his favourite toy is a tennis ball.' Happily, since going to press, this lad has now found his forever home.

I wandered lonely as a Peke
That preens and prances out of doors
When all at once I saw a clique
A host of golden Labradors
Beside the lake, beneath the trees
Cocking their legs upon the breeze.

As ravenous as dogs that dine
Yet hanker after Milky Way
They craned their necks and gave a whine:
Search him for grub! they seemed to say.
Ten thousand saw I at a glance
All eyeing me somewhat askance.

The thought occurred that I should run
Though I was mesmerised indeed
To see such splendour in the sun
And spy so many of my breed:
Yet one idea was uppermost:
Leg it you fool before you're toast.

Now oft when on my bed I lie
Relaxed and chilled in pensive mood
They flash upon my inward eye
When I am thinking of my food
And then my heart with pleasure soars
And dances with the Labradors.

Apologies to William Wordsworth, but Peek
 needed a home

8

OBEDIENCE

As you can see from some of the verse stories, rescue dogs are perfectly capable of a high level of obedience. The Hearing Dogs for the Deaf charity, requiring very rigorous training, began with rescue dog recruits, and many wonderful police dogs were previously turned out by their former owners for delinquency.

For most owners who don't need this level of obedience, it is sufficient to aim for a pet that obeys the law and the house rules and comes when called. There are hundreds of training clubs in Britain whose addresses can be obtained from the Kennel Club. These clubs generally accept any dog, mongrel or pedigree, over six months of age, though if you adopt a puppy you should be teaching it the rudiments beforehand yourself, not letting him run wild. Go along to a club and have a look. If you see dogs being literally throttled with choke chains or, worse still, being beaten and teased by people in padded sleeves, think very carefully indeed about enrolling your friend, especially if you think he or she may have been ill-treated. I have heard of tragic cases of dogs that have become savage after physical coercion training. Classes of the right sort can be an invaluable help. What they do is to school the owner in basic confidence at dog-handling so you can go away and train the dog yourself.

TEACHING THE BASICS

The first requirement of all obedience training is to get your dog used to the collar and lead. Pup or adult: it makes no difference. It must get used to this equipment to live in our overcrowded country and it is an offence to walk a dog along a designated highway *without* a collar, identification tag and lead. If you adopt an adult, it may well have worn them before. A puppy will find it all very strange. Put the collar on in the house for brief periods for a few days and go about your business. Ignore the rebellion: he will soon get used to it provided the collar is not too tight (two-finger room). Mother hippos train their babies to swim by knocking them off the bank and letting them get on with it and, by and large, animals make less fussy parents than we do. That's the first lesson. All the other lessons are based on the principle:

Demonstrate, Repeat, Reward

The worst enemy of anyone trying to train a dog is confusion, so be clear at every stage. Have one person teaching the dog, not half a dozen. Use few words and simple sounds that will make the association in the dog's mind, then lots of praise because rescue dogs may not have heard very much of that in this world.

'NO'

You can usually stop a dog in *flagrante delicto* by making a loud noise. Say 'No! *No!*' loudly and harshly, dropping the pitch of your voice if you can. A metal tray banged against the wall makes a good accompaniment, which is very mysterious and alarming to an unruly dog (don't do this, of course, if you've adopted a very nervous critter). When he associates the act with the racket, he will desist. Smacking, on the other hand, is generally *in*effective. A rescue dog will simply associate this with past cruelty, which didn't in any case reform its behaviour to the owner's satisfaction, but instead made the dog mistrustful and scared. Let repetition and patience be your watchwords.

GETTING USED TO THE LEAD

Most of the larger dog charities walk the dogs in their shelters and therefore get them used to collars and leads. But a few of the smaller, ramshackle ones do not. Collar and lead work is a vital teaching aid. A quick jerk on the lead is an effective form of training – better than smacks, sticks or rolled-up newspapers, all of which keep the dog out of range and repel it from you. Training requires close contact, and there is no point in ordering a dog to do something if you're not in a position to enforce it. The lead is your hotline to the dog's brain.

Get a youngster used to wearing one by clipping it gently to his collar in the house and letting him run up and down under your supervision – keep an eye on him as the lead may catch on something. Chewing can be deterred by dabbing lemon juice on the leather. The next step is to hold the lead at arm's length, backing away and proffering a titbit, which will introduce the queer (to the dog) 'lead feeling' without wrenching the animal up and down. Keep the lessons short and sweet. An adult unused to a lead may be introduced in the same way, but have his lessons in the garden where he can buck without breaking anything. Don't be exasperated because you think these are rudimentary 'puppy' lessons for a grown dog. It may be completely new to him.

The alternative to a choke chain, Dr Roger Mugford's Halti, comes with fitting and teaching instructions and is worn round the dog's head like a halter with the lead attached. This, too, takes some getting used to and should be tried out in the garden, with the dog running up and down on the lead until he forgets his indignation. There is also a leather slip collar, available from most good pet shops, that will control a big dog more kindly than a choke chain if you are really stuck.

HEEL

Stand your dog on your left, lead in your right hand across your body. Hustle the dog firmly up and down, talking to him merrily. If he won't budge, use a titbit as an interim measure (but don't go mad with titbits or you'll have a fat dog). If he pulls ahead, which is much more likely, give a jerk on his collar and say 'Heel!' There's no need to wrench the dog over in a backward somersault; you'll find that if you walk briskly and make a lot of right turns, you'll automatically be in the driving seat and he'll have to pay attention to your movements. These should be short lessons, but you may have to repeat them over and over again because it's quite hard for a rescue dog to understand that he must now keep pace with a human. Some mongrels can never be bothered with precision heel work because they get bored, but so long as you can train the dog not to drag you to destruction, you have achieved the main object of the exercise.

SIT

Even the most dominant, unreclaimed adult relies on you for his food, and you should use this to demonstrate your authority.

At mealtimes, hold the dog's bowl in one hand above his nose and command him to 'Sit!' Say it as though you mean it. If you have him backing away with his rear end against a wall, he will feel physically inclined to sit down anyway; otherwise use your free hand to show him what you mean, pressing down firmly on his hindquarters near the tail. No sit, no din-dins. Be firm. The food method of teaching the 'sit' is better than the lead method, pulling the dog's head up, because it offers a real reward. Pups will be fed three or four times a day, so you will have plenty of practice at instilling your authority.

STAY

This is a continuation of the 'sit', reinforced with a hand signal. If the dog gets up, make him sit down again and say 'Sit – stay!' very firmly. This is not 'teasing' the dog but capturing his entire attention at the moment when you have the most natural control over him – as his dinner-giver. It establishes in his mind that you are the giver of good things and must be listened to, and if you make it a daily routine, the dog will begin to obey you in other ways.

DOGS LEFT ALONE

Many dogs start barking and gnawing when left on their own, and some dogs that have ended up in shelters have been evicted by their owners for this very reason. A dog should be perfectly all right on his own for three or four hours while you go out, provided he has water to drink and a Kong toy to chew – and so long as you have taken a tiny bit of trouble over his training.

The method is simple. After he has gone to the toilet, calmly put the dog or pup in another room and shut the door. Go about your business, but listen for sounds of showing off or destruction. If there's a racket, bang loudly on the door and shout 'Ugh! Bad dog!' and if necessary make a great show of thundering in the room and shaming the treachery. The first lesson might last five minutes, the next ten, and so on. Work up gradually until you can leave the animal on his own for a couple of hours with complete confidence. This is training without tears, because the dog will resign himself to your absence and very probably go to sleep.

As a general rule, *over*-attachment and possessiveness will inevitably cause problems in an owner's relationship with a dog, so love him devotedly but try not to become a clinging couple. Clinging dogs make their own lives a misery and feel so lonely when left that they will defecate, drink out of the toilet bowl, tear, gnaw and howl to show you their feelings. Avoid such habits by the behind-closed door technique. If you can't face the discipline involved, consider a budgie. Dogs are like us: they express their worries in bad ways.

DOWN – STAY
Once your dog has learned to 'sit' and 'stay' for his dinner, he will sit on command on the lead and he will know that 'stay' means to keep still. If you wish to extend his repertoire, you can now teach him 'down', which is fairly easy. From the sit position, casually pull his forelegs from under him so that he is lying instead

of sitting, and say 'Down – stay!' Repeat it a few times – he may keep getting up, so be lavish with your praise when he obeys you. Reinforce the 'stay' by attaching a Flexi-lead or training cord to your dog's collar and backing away with your palm extended, increasing the distance little by little and returning to praise him profusely if he remains down. Once you're sure he's steady, you can throw caution to the wind and try it without any lead at all, but in the garden or an enclosed space at first in case he's crafty.

COME

In this lesson, rather than you returning to the dog, your dog comes to you. Have him on the long lead, walk away from him quietly and when you reach the extent of the lead, turn and face him. Call his name, say 'Come!' in a delighted, cheerful voice, and give a friendly tug on the lead if he needs any encouragement. When he reaches you, praise him a good deal because this is a wonderful thing for a dog to learn. Always bend down to praise him – don't let him jump up, not even a little puppy. Jumping can injure children and elderly people and the habit usually sets in because the dog has been encouraged to leap into someone's arms as a pup. Forewarned is forearmed.

Millie the Bearded Collie was adopted by Emma's owner Annie Christie from a rescue centre in Lincolnshire. She and her brother had been used for breeding and then discarded, the owners having decamped to Spain. 'Millie is typical of the breed – slightly neurotic. She gets scared of the sound of drills, hoovers and mowers and will run and hide. Our other dogs all love a game of ball, but Millie finds it hard to locate a ball because of her fringe.'

You should practise 'come', 'down' and 'stay' many times on the extended lead before you practise without it, or free. The 'come' requires great patience, and lessons should always take place well away from traffic or livestock. If the dog takes ages to come to you, don't smack or scold him when he finally obeys. This will make the association in the dog's mind of 'come – wallop' instead of 'come – glad'. The usual response to a refusal to come should not be to chase the dog or try to stalk up on it, but to turn on your heels and start to walk away, if necessary with a titbit.

That's more or less the Green Cross Code for rescue dogs. If you are more ambitious, try kindly classes, but you can do a good deal at home by remembering that the dog is dependent on you for food, shelter and affection. As Dr Roger Mugford teaches his clients, attachment can be manipulated to your own and your pet's advantage. Owners with problem dogs frequently find it strange when they are told that often doing nothing is just as effective as doing *something*. This is why, when your dog refuses to come, the best method is not to go hounding after it, but to start walking away. And why, when you come home, you establish your authority in his mind by not making a fuss of him until he is calm. A dog's need to be loved is greater than its fear of chastisement. Diversion is better than whacking. Holding the food bowl in the air is better than a confrontation of wills. You have the greatest conceivable advantage over your dog – your brain. You don't need to go fifteen rounds with him.

Kim

Kim belonged to Jon and Anne Hunt in Gosfield, Essex. Says Jon: 'So many people let him down. He was anxious at first – ate a whole half a pound of butter! Love and loyalty grew. He became a good friend of our Labrador Paddy, and eventually they shared the Top Dog position. As an old boy, Kim suffered a severe stroke. We thought the end was near, but seeing us on what we thought was our final visit to the vet to say goodbye, he rallied and enjoyed another six months with us. We feel he is still here.'

Kim looked yet again in their bowls.
Nothing. No food. No water. Mistress gone.
A carer who did not care –
And he had already lost one home,
Barking his anguish in the night:
Somebody come! Somebody come!
Nature made Mongrels stern
To bear often bitter blows,
To lead often loveless lives;
But hardness and harshness take their toll
Of even the brave with an empty bowl.
Just as skylarks and poets soar
High above a humble start
By listening hard and sensing far,
Mongrels too can raise the bar
Though all seems lost and all hope gone
Extending a nose towards a star.
So when the special visitor left
Kim made a final bid supreme
To break his bonds and hunt his dream
And he followed far in the tracks of the car
For miles and days through storm and hail,
With never a flag or a wag of his tail
Until at last Kim and the man
Were reunited in the rain
Never to be lost again.
And Kim went home and as was due
One humble Mongrel dream came true.

Feather

'My darling Feather', Jilly Cooper's gentle black greyhound, was given a life of love and luxury by the writer after he was abandoned at the end of his cruel racing career. He had been left to roam the streets in a tight muzzle that embedded in his face and prevented him from eating. Found in a pitiful state, skeletal and shivering, he was taken to Co. Offely sanctuary in the Irish Midlands and nursed back to health by the owner Dr Mary Jane Fox. Feather then landed on his paws, as he was adopted by the famous Jilly and her husband Leo. He lived to a ripe old age, commandeering the sofa for his snoozing. Thankfully his former owner Paul Nolan was traced and prosecuted, the first such conviction under the new Animal Welfare Act.

I'm such a gentle boy, yet full of zest
I run and leap and twizzle with the best.
I'm what you call intense
Which means I feel strong sense
And wear my heart upon my nose
Which winds your arm round like a snake
So if you're going, you me take
And if you're staying, you me hold
To keep me comfort from the cold.
I'm very shocked by noise and cars
Still tender from my past
When I was roaming street to street
A muzzle squeezing shut my jaws:
I could not speak. I could not eat
And did not think I'd last.
Now I am cuddled up and warm
Allowed to sprint round in mad fits
Allowed to nuzzle with the cats
Who sleep with me and blend around my form.
I do look like a wiggly eel
Or like a panther who grew long and skinny.
My thighs resemble kangaroos'
Though much more thinny but still strong
To drive me all along.
My owner praises all she can
And says I am her gentleman:
A quiet fellow on the whole:
A quiet fellow with a soul.
And yet for all the love I have
And all the fun I feel
I keep that sadness in my gaze
That looked out on my former days
And hope that now is real.

9

BEHAVIOUR BEYOND BEARING

Most rescue dogs are not warmongers but peace-loving animals that have simply lost their homes. Many have come into the shelters through no fault of their own, because their owners have split up, or died, or gone into sheltered housing. But some sadly have been frightened, and some have been cruelly abused. These dogs will need the gift of time to put the past behind them and regain their trust.

Many of the dogs featured in this collection have been rehabilitated from a very bad start and turned into loving and friendly pets (retaining natural naughtiness where possible). So it can be done, and you can do it. But you need to understand 'where the dog is coming from'.

AGGRESSION

Adopted dogs, because they come to regard their owners as saviours rather than just good friends, are prone to aggressive loyalty and jealousy. Usually this causes few problems, other than to make their owners rather conceited. However, sometimes this possessiveness causes belligerent behaviour towards other animals and other people. In this case, it always helps to lower the temperature of your relationship with the dog and share it with friends and neighbours willing to lend a hand. Very often jealous behaviour has been secretly encouraged by the owner, who finds it rather flattering at first.

Don't hug the animal to you every time someone approaches or enters the room. Encourage it to have friendly exchanges with others. Show it that the world will not actually end if you leave it alone for half an hour. Don't create a 'can't cope' dog, and don't become a desperate couple. If your adopted one sees another dog while out on the lead, don't drag it away down the road as though it were a psychopath. If it barks at the 'rival', wait it out, talking soothingly until it shuts up. Let it meet its own kind. Otherwise it may form the impression 'four legs bad, two legs good'. Its behaviour may well be motivated by a desire to protect you and if it thinks you are alarmed, this will confirm its suspicions that you are indeed in danger. Stay calm and friendly.

If you are one of the unlucky few and you find your adopted dog behaving unpleasantly, examine your relationship to see if you have been somehow condoning its antics by your devotion. Your dog's status in the house should be at the bottom of the family pack, beneath your children. Most dogs accept this without much ado because, in the wild, cubs assume the rank of their parents and in wolf packs they are generally born to an august female sired by a leading male. If your dog is unfriendly towards your children, then you must get expert advice. Ask your vet to refer you to an animal behaviourist like Dr Mugford. The best behaviourists have a very high rate of success with healthy dogs that might otherwise be put down for bad conduct. A dog that is aggressive through jealousy and sees a member of your family as a rival for your affections may be helped by having the resented person attending to his feeding and exercise instead of you. A treatment plan of this kind, under expert supervision, can often save the day.

DOG EAT DOG

Status disputes between two *dogs* in the same household can generally be helped by the ruse of favouring the aggressor rather than protecting the underdog. Try it and see. The dogs would have already worked out their mutual status to their own satisfaction by means of dog signs and signals between themselves, and if you try to turn this upside down you will not prevent fights but cause them. Greet the leading dog first, and then the poor little soul to whom your heart goes out. Put the leading dog's lead on first; give him his dinner first. Don't make waves.

Billy ended up at Danaher RSPCA, Wethersfield. Bev Farrell: 'He was just sitting there quietly, looking up with big brown eyes and a sweet sad face.' When they got him home 'he was a nightmare, and nipped my sons as they tried to stop him scavanging in dustbin bags.' Weeks of hell later, Billy was about to go back to the RSPCA. 'But my youngest son was mortified and pleaded with us to give him one more chance. Now Billy is the sweetest dog you could ever meet and very popular in the village. He helps my partner Steve when he's preparing the cricket pitch, loves to attend the matches and really looks forward to the cricket tea.'

There are, in fact, several different types of aggression in dogs, quite apart from the possessive sort, and treatment depends on the cause. The behaviour may have been training-induced, by someone deliberately teasing the dog. It may be pain-induced due to injury or illness, in which case you may need to apply a soft bandage muzzle while the dog is being treated. It may be fear-induced, a not uncommon cause of aggression in problem dogs. The solution is not to rain blows on the animal's head, but to calm its fears, give it a sense of security and gradually desensitise it to the source of terror.

SEXUAL AND TERRITORIAL AGGRESSION

The other common types of aggression are sexual and territorial, the same as with humans. The first may be overcome by neutering – this is *always* preferable to euthanasia or abandonment. The second, territoriality, may be evidenced by the dog causing havoc over intruders such as the gas meter reader or Auntie May. Unfortunately this kind of aggression tends to become reinforced by the fact that many callers, like the postman, go away again rather quickly and the dog thinks this is because he has seen them off. There is really no solution to this kind of 'doorbell behaviour'; indeed you may be very glad of it if you live in a neighbourhood where half the passers-by are casing the joint. Just don't allow your dog to attack legitimate delivery people in the garden.

Dogs who are aggressive towards visitors in the house are usually those who dominate their owners anyway. The animal is simply taking responsibility as housemaster, assuming that his owner is incompetent in these matters. As already mentioned, dogs do not generally enjoy this responsibility. They would much prefer to live in a secure environment with a reliable leader in charge, and they only step in to fill a vacuum. Territorial aggression is therefore often a matter of assuming your natural authority over the dog. Otherwise try shutting the dog in a 'naughty room' at the first sign of bossy behaviour towards a visitor, until he is contrite. After a period in the cooler, he may be very glad of Auntie May's company.

PREY-CHASING

Dogs will instinctively chase that which flees from them – cats, hares, mechanical hares, sheep, fowl, bicycles and even cars. The *movement away* seems to trigger the dog's predatory mechanisms, and a fleeing cat may well be chased whereas a calm, seated cat will often be ignored. This is why even dogs accustomed to cats in the house will frequently chase the same sort of animal in the street or in the garden with unreasoning fervour. Cats are usually quite efficient at escaping, and some will stand at bay and give the dog a taste of their claws to teach him a lesson, but livestock are often not so lucky.

Amber is one of the youngest and most recent additions to Cindy and Tony Hilling's Essex household from the Greyhound Trust. Says Cindy: 'Amber is a singing greyhound who loves the sound of her own voice. She demands your attention.' The pretty brindle sings at certain television programmes and whines during what she considers unnecessary conversations between humans.

I have come across all kinds of 'cures' for livestock-worrying, from shutting the dog in a ram pen to tying a dead chicken to his tail. Obviously, fairly desperate measures are called for if your dog lives in the country and longs to kill sheep and poultry. Many lambs have been mauled by marauding dogs and if yours is caught in the act, he may legally be shot by an irate farmer. The best insight I know into the subject comes from the German war-dog trainer, Konrad Most, who was admittedly rather cruel in his methods. However, observe his reasoning. He says that if a dog is to be prevented from killing a chicken, *the correction must be given at the time when the dog has the intention of doing so.* Loud noise, a water-pistol, a citronella spray (which can be incorporated in a dog's collar – ask at the pet shop), a can of stones thrown down noisily *beside* the dog's head – all these unpleasant stimuli can be associated in the dog's mind with the close proximity of a chicken *before* the dog has actually attacked the chicken.

You may adapt this method, without using corporal punishment, for cats, sheep or any other creature liable to be killed by your adopted dog, by showing him the animal at close quarters while he is on the lead and chastising him very severely before he has murdered anything. If you live near a farm, there may be a sympathetic farmer only too keen to give you a hand in this worthy cause.

GREYHOUND – CALMING

Greyhounds are a special case in point. Some racing dogs are trained using extremely cruel and (to the dog) memorable methods to chase rabbits and hares. Lack of enthusiasm for the task may well result in extreme punishment, abandonment or death. Greyhounds can be successfully rehabilitated and taught not to chase, and a good many go on to live quite happily in homes with cats (and even share their beds). But chasers *must* be re-trained, and this requires understanding and patience. The Greyhound Trust are the acknowledged experts in this field, and will offer advice on which of their dogs are safe with cats and other small animals, and what methods to use to re-train the others. Tens of thousands of ex-racing greyhounds have been re-homed and calmed down from the job they used to do, and they make beloved and gentle family pets.

DESTRUCTION AND DIGGING

Digging in the garden is perfectly natural in dogs; in the wild they are whelped underground and bitches have long racial memories of den-digging. Bone burial is another relic of the canine past. Either fence off the flowerbeds or resign yourself. It can't be 'cured'. Destruction in the house, though, is rather different, and it usually occurs for one of two reasons: boredom associated with lack of exercise, or desperation and distress at being left alone in the house. Obviously, the first is remedied by more exercise. The best answer to the latter is 'alone' training, described earlier. Milder forms of the disease can usually be helped by leaving the radio on when you go out, and 'barking-to-absent-friends' can sometimes be stopped by judicious use of a water-pistol. Go out of the front door and listen. If barking ensues, rush back in and give the dog a good squirt.

Bracken is one of the thirteen Hilling Hounds of Essex and their only Lurcher. He was born in 2006 and has lived on the edge ever since, racing round the paddock obstacle course, diving through the cloth sausage, hurling himself after balls and grabbing visitors by the shoulders for a quick waltz. The Hillings describe him as 'a real live wire who likes to be the life and soul of the party. Always up to mischief and a very happy dog who loves his family.' It is unlikely that he will ever tire.

BIN-BAG RAKING AND WHINING

Some rescue dogs are inveterate scavengers because they have had to feed themselves to survive. If they are allowed to go out unattended they will go through garbage quite shamelessly – bitches as well as dogs. The answer is simple. Don't let your dog out without you. If he whines up a storm after reasonable exercise, get very cross indeed. Tell him that if you have any more of his nonsense you'll take him to the vet's to be *attended to* in the undercarriage department. Then ignore him altogether. When he sees he can't attract your attention by showing off, he will desist.

MUCK-ROLLING

Some rescue dogs are fervent ordure-rollers, dropping their shoulders to many offensive substances in fields and forests and emerging with unspeakable stink-coats. I have no idea how to cure this, but may I suggest a plastic mac?

Barney

Barney, now thirteen, was given a home six years ago by Mary and Gary Martin after his owner, Gary's dad, emigrated to Spain. Mary: 'We were pleased to take him on,' though Barney had certain naughty ways. He would slyly sleep on their bed while they were out and if they came home early 'he would come down the stairs grumbling and growling.' He knocks the phone off the hook if it rings and will not tolerate the theme tunes of TV soaps – he starts barking. 'He wants non-stop stroking and will nudge you if you tire.'

A steady dog am I:
Not in a flurry.
I never fight or fly
Or whine or worry.
I see a lot of other dogs
Get in a lather
Barking and brawling in the sun.
That's why I'd rather
Be just a steady dog.

A steady dog am I:
What's past is perished.
I don't look back and cry
For what I cherished.
I see a lot of rescue dogs
Sorrowing over those they knew
But I'm just glad I'm here with you
To be your steady dog.

Herbert

Annie Christie of Gosfield in Essex, Herbert's owner: 'His name is very apt. He is a feisty little boy, but he was very sweet and supportive when I lost my dear dog Emma. Herbie came to us very hand-shy. If you put your hand out to stroke him he would snap at your fingers. You must watch him with other dogs because he gets himself in fight mode. He loves Bonzo and cuddles up to him, but he will occasionally latch on to Bonzo's ear, in case he wants a fight. Poor Bonzo doesn't – he is very subservient – but Bert is just checking.'

I'm not having that.
Their blasted cockerel fluttering at me.
So I snarl up a storm.
That shuts him up. That fixes him, all right.
No, I'm not having that.
I'm not having crows, rooks, riffraff
On my land. Or rats rooting about.
I snuffle them all out.
One snap and it's good night.
Gone with one bite, as I'm not having that.
Shepherd Dog Bonzo?
He's allowed to live
Here in my house. I warn him now and then
By latching on his ear.
He's never piped up once.
No fear. He knows just what he'd get
As I'm not having that.
Dogs in the street I've met?
I look them in the eye.
'Want a trip to the vet?' I say.
And then I just let fly, as I'm not having that.
They got me out of Battersea
Especially to run this farm.
Sharing that tractor with my Dad.
Yes, I worked hard – I did my part.
That's why I'm boss. And yet I've got a heart.
Not an unfeeling chap, no. Not a cad.
When we lost my Mum's olden dog
Missus got very sad.
I said as I jumped on her lap:
'Don't worry Mum – You've still got me.
You see? It's not all bad.'

10

DOGS MOST ABANDONED

BRITAIN'S
MOST ABANDONED
BREED

THE MONGREL

When I began writing dog books years ago, the most abandoned breed was not a 'breed' at all. The mongrel was the traditional working-class dog, and thousands of them roamed the streets before there was any legislation to prevent them, meeting and mating with other mongrels or any 'pure-bred' dog who happened to feel available.

Mongrels were therefore very numerous and very cheap, and many were regarded as canine riffraff, easily obtained and even more easily disposed of. Shelters up and down the country were full of them, despite the fact that mongrels are among the most intelligent, individual, resourceful and talented animals on earth. One of my own dog books *The Mongrel* (Popular Dogs, 1985) detailed some of their history and numerous unsuccessful attempts, such as London's annual Dog Whipping Day and a scheme by Victorian show judge Major Harding Cox, to wipe out 'the gamin of the gutter' altogether.

Many of us who have had the honour of owning a mongrel have become their standard-bearers, and I was proud to be one of the original organisers of the National Mongrel Show *Scruffts* – the non-pedigree equivalent of Crufts – that was held for many years at Hewitts Farm near Orpington in Kent. Our hundreds of contestants, competing for such prestigious titles as Best Bone Finder and Best Lamp-post User, came from as far away as Wales and Scotland, and owners were as proud of their dogs as any Crufts winner. We received a great deal of positive publicity and the whole thing snowballed. In the end the show became so unwieldy that we asked the RSPCA to take it over as a fund-raising event. It has now been incorporated into Crufts as a 'Crossbreed' competition, implying that all mongrels derive from pedigrees. Rubbish!

In Britain's shelters today there are still a good many mongrels (the progeny of other mongrels) and crossbreeds (with at least one known pedigree parent and not just a passing resemblance to a particular breed), and some of our featured dogs are of this esteemed type. But times have changed. If you ask animal welfare people these days what are the most abandoned breeds, you get different answers. There are regional variations: in Wales, for example, the

Bran's owner Michelle Hailey found him nine years ago at Margaret Aldridge's very happy and well-run little shelter in White Colne, Essex. But being dumped at six months for not resembling a whippet had given Bran attitude, and phobias about thunder, bang noises, kittens, cows, cameras and statues of animals. A 'tornado' indoors, he also 'pulled up plants, dug holes and ate his dog leads and collars. He left presents of poo on the floor, usually containing a free plastic toy that he had devoured.' Castration and a Lurcher pal, Celt, saved the day. Says Michelle: 'He has made our lives very happy and we couldn't wish for better dogs.'

most abandoned breed is probably the Border Collie. Elsewhere, two breeds vie for the title of Britain's Biggest Castaway. They are, for very different reasons, the Greyhound and the Staffie.

THE GREYHOUND

A good number of the rescue dogs featured in this book, you will have noticed, are greyhounds. This is partly because I've had a greyhound myself. To own one is to fall in love with the breed, and my beautiful blue boy Jo and his great tenth birthday adventure are described in one of the poems. My friends Cindy and Tony Hilling, who have given their lives to greyhound rescue and cruelty cases, have at any one time a dozen of these loveable dogs sharing their home, who are full of hope and affection despite their bad experiences. Some of the Hilling Hounds have been mentioned in this book, and on the Facebook page of my present rescue Parson Russell Terrier named Owen Parsnip, you will find many more retired greyhounds from all over the world celebrated enormously. A lot of them speak 'greylish', a kind of doggie gibberish that is fairly intelligible and very imaginative. To greyhound rescuers these dogs are treasures beyond price, worth far more than they ever earned by winning at the races.

The other reason for featuring these particular dogs in a rescue book is that greyhounds are one of the country's two most abandoned breeds (the other being the Staffie). They are overbred and readily disposed of, and many come from Ireland with green identity numbers tattooed in their ears that you can look up on the internet to discover the dog's history and racing success.

In 2015 the Greyhound Trust was proud to home its 75,000th greyhound. Each year approximately eight thousand greyhounds 'retire' (or are discarded) from racing, and the GT finds homes for about half of these. This means that there are four thousand of these elegant, graceful and gentle dogs in need of a loving home each year, sadly staring through the bars of their kennels. No dog ever looks quite as sad as a limpid-eyed greyhound staring into space.

Yet they are not difficult dogs; far from it. As the Greyhound Trust explains on its website, 'A greyhound is the original low-maintenance companion animal. They are intelligent and affectionate, laid back and docile. They only need two short walks a day and will happily spend the rest of their time dozing by your side.'

If you think you might like to give a greyhound a home, here is a Q & A from the GT's website that offers some inside information.

GREYHOUND Q & A

Q. Are greyhounds highly strung?

A. *No. They are naturally calm, noble and elegant.* They are the oldest dog breed recorded in history and are genuine thoroughbreds.

Q. Are greyhounds good with children, the elderly and other dogs?

A. *Greyhounds are as good with children as any dog breed, and better than most because of their characteristic gentleness. They have been around people all of their lives and are usually very people-oriented. Their low maintenance requirements and temperament make them the perfect companion for the elderly. Most greyhounds get on well with other dogs and many live with other breeds. Common sense and careful introductions are the key. If you have another dog, speak to our volunteers who will usually recommend that you bring the animal down to the kennels to help pick their new greyhound friend.*

Q. Are there character differences between males and females?

A. *The difference between male and female greyhounds tends to be less pronounced than in many other breeds. There are though a far higher number of male greyhounds currently awaiting homing within our kennels due to their greater numbers in the racing industry.*

Q. How much exercise do they need?

A. *Contrary to popular belief, greyhounds do not need lots of exercise. Toilet considerations aside, two twenty minute walks a day is usually more than enough. Greyhounds are built for speed, not stamina, and use up their energy in short bursts.*

Q. Do they always need to be muzzled?

A. *Greyhounds do not need to be muzzled at all times, but we do recommend that you keep your greyhound muzzled when out and about, at least until you are confident of their behaviour around other breeds. They are quite used to it and associate it with pleasurable walks. If you feel you need to let your dog off the lead, a confined space and the wearing of a muzzle is recommended. We provide a collar, lead and muzzle with every greyhound that we home.*

Q. Will I need a special bed for the dog?

A. *Greyhounds do not need a special bed, and an old, clean quilt folded in two is perfect. They are used to sleeping off the ground and will need no encouragement to take over your bed as well as your sofa. They do like to stretch out!*

Q. Can greyhounds live with cats and other small pets?

A. *Greyhounds are sighthounds and it is their instinct to chase. Despite this, some greyhounds can be trained to live happily with cats and other small pets (and sometimes they even become the best of friends!). If you have a cat or another small pet, make sure to discuss this with your local branch who will be able to let you know if they have any greyhounds that they think will be suitable.*

GREYHOUND MEDICAL INSURANCE

To get them started on the right path, every greyhound homed through the Greyhound Trust receives four weeks' free insurance from Petplan. Petplan Covered for Life® policies renew the vet fee benefit each year for the rest of your pet's life provided the policy is renewed each year with no break in cover. This scheme means that you can adopt the greyhound best suited to your own lifestyle with the peace of mind that you'll be covered for any future health challenges.

THE STAFFIE

The Staffordshire Bull Terrier has for generations been one of Britain's best-loved and most popular breeds. But when vicious British yobs began to breed and train dogs on a large scale for aggression, the Dangerous Dogs Act was introduced to try to control Pit Bull Terriers and similar *looking* breeds. Since then, Staffies have suffered a very bad press indeed.

Isolated tragic incidents in which individual dogs, cruelly trained for fighting, have attacked children and subsequently been destroyed, have been generalised to demonise the entire breed, including many thousands of perfectly innocent and harmless dogs. The British Veterinary Association and welfare organisations have pleaded for the dangerous dogs legislation – which has in any case failed to curb the breeding of Pit Bulls – to be reframed on the basis of what they call 'deed not breed'. In other words, attacks should be seen as the work of individual dogs rather than the fault of whole breeds. No dog should be judged and killed

Bridgend Dogs' Trust (01656 724 598): 'Mr Tumnus is about six years old and can be temperamental at times. Once he gets to know you he overcomes his grumpiness and likes to cuddle up and bond. When he first came to us he was very worried and reactive but now that he trusts the staff he can be quite sweet – he'll do almost anything for a tasty treat.' He needs an adult-only home with no other dogs, and his new owners would need to be experienced with Staffie-types and to visit Mr T a few times before adopting him.

simply on the basis of what it *looks* like, though this is often the sole criterion in many destruction orders at the moment.

Any dog, even a Pug or a Yorkie, is capable of aggression and biting. Some dogs are larger or more powerful than others and their bites can therefore be more serious. Generally speaking, if dogs are trained by mindless thugs to bite and fight, they will. But the vast majority of dogs live placidly with us, and the Staffie is no exception.

One of the most abandoned breeds in the UK, the Staffordshire Bull Terrier or 'Staffie' has suffered from a toxic mix of terrible cruelty by dog-fighting criminals and rotten publicity. Now commonly regarded as a 'devil dog' by sections of the media, the Staffie has been maligned as a vicious breed unsuitable for the family home. Yet for generations of Staffordshire potters who originally produced the breed for dog-fighting, the Staffie was always regarded as 'the Nanny Dog' and required to live and sleep in their crowded hovels with their children. Any sign of aggression towards humans was beaten and bred out of the Staffie by the potters until, as dog behaviourist Stan Rawlinson points out, 'They were trusted so much that it was common to see an injured fighting dog covered in blood taken back home in the same pram as the newest babies.' Odd that people will now cross over the road rather than walk past one of the breed.

The Staffordshire Bull Terrier was recognised by the Kennel Club in 1935, one hundred years after the Humane Act banned bear and bull-baiting. Its breed standard and description is one of only two that states the dog must be 'totally reliable' and suitable with young children. So how come such a loyal and loving family dog, officially described as 'totally loving to its family', should have earned the modern reputation of canine murderer?

Lisa Richards, RSPCA dog welfare expert, said: 'Staffies have suffered a great deal from overbreeding and bad press in recent years and, unfortunately, many end up with rescue organisations due to irresponsible ownership or because their owners were unable to cope with having a dog. Sadly, lots of people still buy a dog without doing any research or considering the responsibilities involved, resulting in many dogs ending up with charities.

'Improving responsible ownership and encouraging people to do research before getting a dog, so they are informed and prepared for the commitment of having a pet, will hopefully help improve the outlook for Staffies, along with offering help on training and behaviour to resolve any problems should they occur. The RSPCA are also campaigning for a properly enforced licensing regime to help ensure that all puppies are bred and reared in a way that gives them the best chance of living happy, healthy lives.

'Staffies do not deserve the bad reputation they often receive and, just like any dog, given the right upbringing and care, can make loving, rewarding pets and many of the Staffies in our care would suit a range of different families.'

Stan Rawlinson points out on his website *The Dog Listener* that attacks on humans are often the work of Staffie-crosses, where the breeder has deliberately altered the dog's loving temperament to make it aggressive towards humans by interbreeding with other banned bull breeds, 'watering down or removing the strong anti-aggressive human bond.'

But the very loyalty of the Staffie has been mercilessly exploited by morons who make money from illegal dog-fights. These criminals consider honing a dog as a weapon enhances their pitiful status. The League Against Cruel Sports who investigate the fights have published the following statement on the 'depraved' owners who force bull breeds, Staffies and any other potentially powerful and fearless dog to do as they say: 'Innocent dogs are being engineered to kill, and their handlers will stop at nothing to give them the competitive edge. Fights range from impromptu one-on-one street "rolls", to professional, organised fights with high-stakes gambling involved.' The LACS highlight the following brutal 'training' methods:

- Being forced to run on treadmills for several hours a day, and to hang for hours at a time from tyres suspended from tree branches.

- 'Body slamming' – where a person sits on the dog's body for up to two hours and punches it every time it moves.

- 'Head slamming' – where the dog's head is violently slammed into a wall to harden the skull.

- Using bait animals. In the early stages, small animals such as rabbits or kittens are used, and later, cats and small dogs. Some of these animals will be stolen family pets. Most will end up being ripped to shreds.

The League has found that the canine gladiators 'are robbed of their natural instincts and engineered to ignore their own suffering. For example, they learn not to scream, even when in agonising pain. And of course serious injury is inevitable. But they will not receive any pain relief or veterinary treatment.' And as if that were not bad enough, 'Those who survive the fight will often die later from their appalling injuries or from shock. Those who lose will often be killed as punishment for bringing shame to their handler, or for losing them money. In these cases the killing is particularly violent, such as being beaten to death in front of other dogs to terrify them.'

The League Against Cruel Sports urges everybody to join their online petition to put a stop to this barbaric cruelty. And I urge every reader to consider whether Staffies, those most despised and discarded of dogs, may have shouldered the blame for the much more dangerous creatures behind the fights.

THE 'ALVIN' PERSONALITY
Staffies that have *not* been deliberately bred, goaded and trained for aggression, are loving, funny characters who make excellent family pets. 'Alvin', one of our featured dogs, is a very good example of the normal Staffie personality – their main motivation in life is simply to please, protect and entertain their people. Yet these strong-willed though perfectly trainable and affectionate animals are being abandoned in their thousands by excessively safety-conscious families who 'fear the worst', even from dogs that have lived harmlessly with them for years.

Go to the average rescue shelter these days and you'll see them – Staffie after Staffie, large and small, in cage after cage and row after row, sitting there in their little pens with their miserable faces full of despair at humankind and their eyes searching you for the missing piece of this puzzle. *Why am I here? What have I done?* The sight is heartbreaking.

A BBC Television *Panorama* (aired on 2 August 2010) examined the crisis of dog abandonment in the UK and highlighted the plight of the Staffie. Of the 8,000 dogs Battersea received in 2009, an extraordinary 3,600 were Staffies, and this growing rate of abandonment is reflected throughout the country. Several of the dogs actually destroyed during the programme were Staffies who showed no evident aggression towards anyone.

If you have any experience at all with strong-willed breeds, please consider a Staffie for rescue. The shelter owners usually know a good deal about the dogs they house and the larger rescue organisations can help you choose a safe and suitable character for your home and even help you with his or her training.

MORE ABOUT THE BREED

Lesley McFadyen

Secretary – EASBTC
(East Anglia Staffordshire Bull Terrier Club)

The Staffordshire Bull Terrier was recognised as a pure breed by the Kennel Club in 1935, being a mix of the Bulldog of the time and the English White Terrier. As one of only two breeds whose Breed Standard states suitability with children, it is known as a great family dog. The Stafford temperament should always be totally bombproof with people, although they are not always so reliable around other dogs or animals due to their baiting heritage. That said, many Staffords can and do live with other dogs, but owners should always be 'one step ahead'. What can begin as play can end in disaster, therefore 'getting another one for company' shouldn't be seen as an option.

In the 1990s the popularity of the breed peaked, with more than twelve thousand puppies per year being registered as well as large numbers of unregistered pups being bred. As breed exploitation rose, numbers of Staffords and their crosses in rescue situations increased. The Stafford isn't the right breed for everyone, and the first year of raising a Stafford pup can be very challenging; they are lively and often headstrong pups that need consistent guidelines and training. They crave human company so are not a breed to own if being left for long periods.

Numbers of Kennel Club (KC) registered Staffords have dropped considerably (4,500 in 2015) but still large numbers of unregistered dogs, including crosses, fill the 'pups for sale' ads. Currently the 'blue' colour accounts for in excess of 65 per cent of KC registered pups in 2015, having been marketed as a 'rare' colour by unscrupulous breeders selling for inflated prices. The blue gene in Staffords is dilute, and it is unwise to breed with another dilute gene, but fashion dictate has seen this exploited, meaning that traditional colours of the Stafford (red, fawn, brindle, black and white) are in serious decline and are in danger of being overcome completely. No doubt in the future, dog rescuers will see a sharp increase in blue Staffords seeking new homes.

Staffords don't fare well in a kennel situation. Enjoying human company so much, they find the isolation of a kennel environment very stressful. Many Staffords in rescue kennels develop behavioural issues and show extreme stress, meaning they don't show their most appealing side when people are looking with a view to offering a home. Fortunately some dog rescuers use foster care, giving a better understanding of the individual dog.

One dog that's gone from being rescued to a hero is 'Stella the Staffie', abandoned at West Hatch RSPCA kennels, Taunton and taken on by

Gloucestershire Police as a drugs, cash and ammunition search dog. Stella won the Animal Hero of the Year Award in 2015 for finding £25,000. Gloucestershire Police Force now has five Stafford crosses working for them – an example of turning a dog's life around.

The East Anglian Staffordshire Bull Terrier Display Team consists of home-bred and rescued Staffords, and its staff attends events around the country showing the breed in a positive and entertaining way.

The Staffie is one of the breeds that has suffered most unfairly under the recent Dangerous Dogs Act and Breed Specific Legislation (BSL). But many other innocent dogs have come to grief under its shadow of execution, which works with the same mind-boggling injustice as the witch-finding laws of the 1640s under Matthew Hopkins. So draconian is BSL that in 2014 a cross-breed known as Tyson, a trained police detection dog, was found guilty of belonging to the banned 'Pitbull type'. Officers at Avon and Somerset Police had taken Tyson, an eighteen-month-old dark brindle and white Pitbull-cross, after he had appeared with distinction on Channel 5's show *The Dog Rescuers* and was making great progress with his training. But a police dog specialist ruled that, despite Tyson's sweet nature and 'great potential', the dog had to be returned to the West Hatch RSPCA centre near Taunton, where no other home could be found for him because of the Government's breed prohibitions. PC Lee Webb, the dog's handler, was appalled and upset. Tyson, who had faithfully served the police and harmed no one, was destroyed. An RSPCA spokesperson commented: 'All the staff who cared for and loved him are incredibly upset that such a wonderful dog had to be put to sleep.'

The following statement has been provided by the RSPCA.

Q. What is Breed Specific Legislation (BSL) and what does it do?

A. BSL is part of a law (the Dangerous Dogs Act 1991) that makes the possession of four types of dog illegal in the UK – the Pit Bull Terrier, Japanese Tosa, Dogo Argentino and Fila Braziliero.

The intention behind this law was to protect people – these types of dogs are traditionally bred for dog fighting, are strong and powerful and could, in the wrong hands, hurt people or other dogs. The government at the time did not want them to be in widespread circulation.

Supporters of the law say that BSL has prevented injuries by keeping these types out of the country – however, experts in this area accept there are probably more Pit Bull Terriers in the UK now than in the late 1980s. Others say that more breeds or types should be added as there are lots of powerful dogs being kept and used inappropriately.

But there is a negative side to the law: BSL can lead to confusion over whether or not particular dogs are prohibited. Dogs that are seized can be kept in kennels for long periods of time, while legal argument is had over whether they are 'substantially of type', which is required to prove a case.

Obviously this can impact on the dog's welfare and unfortunately the law does not allow such dogs to be re-homed.

So where the dog is a nice dog, but happens to be a Pit Bull Terrier, and has an unsuitable owner (e.g. with a long criminal record) the dog has to be euthanised. The courts rarely allow the dog to be 'exempted' to such an owner.

This system therefore is not a good use of public funds, nor is it fair on the dogs or the owners.

BSL also goes against one of the RSPCA's key messages: the focus should be on the other end of the lead – i.e. the owner. This means that any dog can be dangerous in the wrong hands e.g. mistreated or badly trained, regardless of its breed or type. For these reasons, the RSPCA is opposed to BSL and would like to see it abolished.

Mabel

Mabel was rescued by Carol Anderson and Tracey Doyle of Pattiswick in Essex. 'She was roughly two-and-a-half. She had already had two other homes and spent all her time chained.' Initially because of muscle wastage she was 'unable to walk round our garden, let alone further afield.' Now she can do a two-mile hike, has a regular cut and blow dry and loads of cuddles. 'She adores children, in particular our son Thomas, of whom she is very protective.' Despite trips to beaches and rivers, this Newfoundland 'refuses to get her feet wet – you try shifting 55 kilograms.'

Fudge

Fudge shouts out, not sure what it's about.
Bark bark! Something he needs.
His thick silk hair and ears lie flat
Across his head like a matador's hat.
His eyes are eager beads.
Those legs don't fit his form at all:
They'd fit a Yorkie
Or something small but if you call
Him a sawn-off little sprout
It's simply liable to make Fudge shout.
He barks, but his eyes are saying please!
His small paws gripping on your knees
He studies you with fixed intent.
A will of iron - he won't relent.

He stares as his needs are very great.

What is it Fudge? What is that sound?

Hang on. I think I can translate:

Promise don't send me to the pound.

Owen Parsnip

Owen Parsnip and the author met six years ago, soon after the author's Greyhound, Jo, had died. When he first ran over to her, Owen was leadless, scared and filthy, having apparently been left by a van in the nature reserve. Searches by the local dog warden and a posting on the RSPCA's Lost and Found website failed to trace his former owner. Owen now runs the Dog Revolutionary Army on Facebook, with over two hundred and fifty animal soldiers and 1,600 human fans campaigning for dog rights and against 'two-leg oppression'. The organisation has divisions, an anthem and banners, and some members even have helmets.

You see that gap in the clouds
Where the sliver of sun breaks through?
That's you.
You see those spangles on the lake
With the silver rings that the mayflies make?
That's you.
You're the chink of charm in a world of spite,
A warm breath in the long cold night.
And I can't prove love makes us whole
Or therefore that we have a soul
But if I do, you do.

Appendix 1

DOG BANS AND PSPOs

The anti-dog lobby is very well-organised and influential at local council level. On the whole they would prefer dogs to be quietly excluded from public places. In just two years since the introduction of so-called Public Space Protection Orders (PSPOs), dog walking has been banned or severely restricted in more than 3,300 parks and open spaces in Britain. The Kennel Club consulted almost seventy councils to find out what level of restriction was being placed on dogs and their owners under their new powers. While some have imposed targeted bans in areas such as children's playgrounds or sports pitches, on average the councils consulted had 48 separate orders in place restricting dog walking. One had 116.

Caroline Kisco, Secretary of the Kennel Club, warned in the *Daily Telegraph* on 21 January 2017 that some local authorities appeared to be waging a vendetta against dog owners. She said that Britain had long been renowned as a dog-loving nation and dog walkers provide many social benefits as they often act as the eyes and ears of local communities in public places. The Kennel Club do not want all this to be undermined by unfair and unnecessary restrictions that fine and penalise dog owners going about their daily lives.

Under the swingeing powers of PSPOs, dogs have been *completely* banned from at least 2,205 public places including parks, playing fields and beaches in England and Wales. They have also been forbidden from running or playing off a lead in 1,100 others places. Yet under recent welfare legislation, owners are required to provide reasonable exercise, and they also need to socialise their pets if they are not to develop behavioural problems.

According to an RSPCA Spokesperson: 'Dogs enjoy interacting and playing with other people and animals, and it is important that they are able to express normal behaviour off the lead. We realise the value of Public Space Protection Orders for local authorities to ensure that sections of open space, like children's play areas and sports fields, may be dog-free. However, where dogs are excluded or open spaces are restricted, it is essential that local authorities make sure other open spaces are available close by. We hope local authorities issue PSPOs cautiously and do not use them as a blanket power that punishes the responsible majority in an effort to tackle problems created by an irresponsible few.'

Appendix 2

ASSOCIATION OF DOGS AND CATS HOMES: CURRENT MEMBER CHARITIES

Secretary – Peter Laurie c/o Battersea Dogs and Cats Home
4 Battersea Park Road, London, SW8 4AA
secretary@adch.org.uk

The ADCH have a full list of members on their website at:
http://www.adch.org.uk/membership/current-members

Their membership is updated regularly on their website. For your convenience, here is a printed version, accurate at the time of going to press.

ADCH Vice-Presidents
Lt. Col. Duncan Green CBE
Clarissa Baldwin CBE
Dennis Baker, Wood Green Animal Shelters

Elected Officers & Committee
Chairman - Claire Horton, Battersea Dogs & Cats Home
Vice Chairman - Peter Hepburn, Cats Protection
Secretary - Peter Laurie, Battersea Dogs & Cats Home, London
secretary@adch.org.uk
Treasurer - Geoff Wright, Margaret Green Animal Rescue
treasurer@adch.org.uk
Clare Williams, National Animal Welfare Trust

Clive Byles, Wood Green Animal Shelters

David Bowles, RSPCA

Giles Webber, Dogs Trust

Jacquie Neilson, Rain Rescue

Mandy Jones, Blue Cross

Stephen Coleman, Jersey SPCA

Steve Bryne, Guernsey SPCA

Website Administration - Ben Wilkes, Border Collie Trust GB

Full Members

**Abandoned Animals
Association**
Tel: 01745 857975
www.abandonedanimals.org.uk

**Animal Care (Lancaster,
Morecombe & District)**
Tel: 01524 65495
Fax: 01524 841819
www.animalcare-lancaster.co.uk

Animals In Distress
Tel: 01803 812121
Fax: 01803 814 085
www.animalsindistress.uk.com

Ashbourne Animal Welfare
Tel: 01335 300 494
www.ashbourneanimalwelfare.org

Assisi Animal Sanctuary
Tel: 02891 812622
www.assisi-ni.org

Bath Cats & Dogs Homes
Tel: 01225 787321
Fax: 01225 311118
www.bathcatsanddogshome.org.uk

**Battersea Dogs &
Cats Home**
Tel: 020 7627 9203/4
Fax: 020 7627 9200
www.battersea.org.uk

**Bleakholt Animal
Sanctuary**
Tel: 0844 257 0411
www.bleakholt.org

Birmingham Dogs' Home
Tel: 01902 790618 (Sunnyside)
Tel: 0121 643 5211 (Birmingham)
Fax: 0121 6430910 (Birmingham)
www.birminghamdogshome.org.uk

The Blue Cross
Tel: 01993 822651
Fax: 01993 823083
www.bluecross.org.uk

Oak Tree Animals' Charity Carlisle
Tel: 01228 560 082
www.oaktreeanimals.org

Border Collie Trust GB
Tel: 01889 577058
www.bordercollietrustgb.org.uk

Bristol Dogs & Cats Home
Tel: 0117 977 6043
www.rspca-bristol.org.uk

Dogs Trust
Tel: 020 7837 0006
Fax: 020 7833 2701
www.dogstrust.org.uk

Dogs Trust Ireland
Tel: 00 353 18791000
www.dogstrust.ie

Dumfries & Galloway Canine Rescue Centre
Tel: 01387 770210
www.caninerescue.co.uk

Eden Animal Rescue
Tel: 01931 716114
www.edenanimalrescue.org.uk

Edinburgh Dog and Cat Home
Tel: 0131 669 5331
Fax: 0131 657 5601
www.edch.org.uk

English Springer Spaniel Welfare
Tel: 01237 451991
www.englishspringerwelfare.co.uk

Fen Bank Greyhound Rescue
Tel: 01754 820593
www.fenbankgreyhounds.co.uk

Foal Farm Animal Rescue Centre
Tel: 01959 572 386
www.foalfarm.org.uk

Forever Hounds Trust
Tel: 03000 111 100
www.foreverhoundstrust.org

Gables Farm Dogs' and Cats' Home (Plymouth)
Tel: 01752 331 602
Fax: 01752 331 604
www.gablesfarm.org.uk

German Shepherd Rescue Elite
Tel: 01623 798943
www.gsrelite.co.uk

Gloucestershire Animal Welfare Association and Cheltenham Animal Shelter
Tel: 01242 523521
Fax: 01242 523676
www.gawa.org.uk

Greyhound Trust
Tel: 0208 3353016
www.greyhoundtrust.org.uk

Guernsey SPCA
Tel: 01481 257261
Fax: 01481 251 147
www.gspca.org.gg

Halfway Home Dog Rescue
Tel: 0780 800 3152
www.halfwayhome-dogrescue.org

Holly Hedge Animal Sanctuary
Tel: 01275 474719
www.hollyhedge.org.uk

Hope Rescue
Tel: 07545 822919
www.hoperescue.org.uk

HULA Animal Rescue (Bedfordshire Home for Unwanted and Lost Animals)
Tel: 01908 584000
Fax: 01908 282020
www.hularescue.org

ISPCA
Tel: 00353 43 25029
Fax: 00353 43 25024
www.ispca.ie

Jersey SPCA Animals' Shelter
Tel: 01534 724 331
Fax: 01534 871797
www.jspca.org.je

Jerry Green Dog Rescue
Tel: 01652 657820
www.jerrygreendogs.org.uk

The Kennel Club
Tel: 0870 6066750
Fax: 020 7518 1028
www.thekennelclub.org.uk

The Labrador Lifeline Trust
Tel: 01256 884027 / 07860691251
www.labrador-lifeline.co.uk

Labrador Rescue Trust
Tel: 07791 519084
www.labrador-rescue.com/

Leicester Animal Aid
Tel: 01455 888 257
Fax only: 01455 888 550
www.leicesteranimalaid.org.uk

Leitrim Animal Welfare
Tel: 00 353 71964 8300
www.leitrimanimals.com

Lord Whisky Sanctuary Fund
Tel: 01303 862 622
www.lordwhisky.co.uk

Manchester & Cheshire Dogs Homes
Tel: 0871 918 1212
Tel: 0871 918 1212 (Ches)
Fax: 0161 277 6949
www.dogshome.net

Manx SPCA
Tel: 01624 851 672
Tel/Fax: 01624 852 923
www.manxspca.com

Margaret Green Animal Rescue
Tel: 01929 480 474
Fax: 01929 480860
www.margaretgreenanimalrescue.
 org.uk

Mayflower Sanctuary
Tel: 01302 711330
www.mayflowersanctuary.co.uk

Mayhew Animal Home
Tel: 020 8969 0178/7110
Fax: 020 8964 3221
www.themayhew.org

Mrs Murrays Cat and Dog Home
Tel: 01224 483624
Fax: 01224 486165
www.mrsmurrays.co.uk

National Animal Welfare Trust
Tel: 020 8950 0177
Fax: 020 8420 4454
www.nawt.org.uk

Newcastle Dog and Cat Shelter
Tel: 0191 215 0435
Fax: 0191 266 9942
www.dogandcatshelter.com

North Clwyd Animal Rescue
Tel: 01745 560546
www.ncar.org.uk

Pawprints Dog Rescue
Tel: 07415 030165
www.pawprintsdogrescue.org

Porthcawl Animal Welfare Society
Tel: 01656 773307
www.pawsporthcawl.com

Rain Rescue
Tel: 02476 542566 or
Tel: 07415 030165
www.rainrescue.co.uk

Raystede Centre for Animal Welfare
Tel: 01825 840 252
Fax: 01825 840 995
www.raystede.org

RSPCA
Tel: 0300 123 0365
www.rspca.org.uk

RSPCA Liverpool Branch
Tel: 0151 220 3812
Fax: 0151 220 3821
www.rspcaliverpoolbranch.co.uk

Society for Abandoned Animals
Tel: 0161 9735318
www.saarescue.co.uk

St Francis Home For Animals (Newquay)
Tel: 01637 872976
www.stfrancisnewquay.org.uk

Stokenchurch Dog Rescue
Tel: 01494 482695
www.stokenchurchdogrescue.co.uk

Stray Aid
Tel: 0300 999 4247
www.strayaid.org.uk

Teckels Animal Sanctuaries
Tel: 01452 740 300
www.teckels.weebly.com/

Thornberry Animal Sanctuary
Tel: 01909 564399
www.thornberryanimalsanctuary.org

Wood Green
Tel: 0844 248 8181
Fax: 01480 832815
www.woodgreen.org.uk

Woodside Animal Welfare Trust
Tel. 01752 347503
www.woodsidesanctuary.org.uk

Worcestershire Animal Rescue Shelter (WARS)
Tel: 01905 831651
www.wars.org.uk

Associate Members

Airedale Terrier Club of Scotland
Tel: 01241 830 406
www.atcsonline.co.uk

Akita Welfare & Rescue Trust (UK)
Tel: 0845 2602 206

All Dogs Matter
Tel: 020 8341 3196
www.alldogsmatter.co.uk

Animal Concern Cumbria
Tel: 01946 748056
ww.animalconcerncumbria.org

Babbington Rescue CIC
Tel: Tel: 0115 932 4576
www.babbington-rescue.org.uk

Bolton Destitute Animal Shelter
Tel: 01204 526486
www.animalshelter.org.uk

Borders Pet Rescue
Tel: 01896 849090
www.bawa.org.uk

Boxer Welfare Scotland
Tel: 01779 812 799
www.boxerwelfarescotland.co.uk

Bristol Dog Action Welfare Group
Tel: 0117 969 5332
www.dawg.org.uk

Bulldog Rescue
Tel: 0871 200 2450
www.bulldogrescue.co.uk

Dobermanns In Need
Tel: 01243 542545
www.dobermannsinneed.co.uk

Dog Aid Society of Scotland Limited
Tel: 0131 668 3633
www.dogaidsociety.com

Four Paws Animal Rescue
Tel: 07358 398319
www.fourpawsanimalrescue.org.uk

Freshfields Animal Rescue
Tel: 0151 931 1604
www.freshfieldsrescue.org.uk

Great Dane Adoption Society
Tel: 01205 481 248
www.danes.org.uk

Greyhound Welfare
Tel: 01633 892 846
www.greyhoundwelfare.org.uk

Grovehill Animal Trust
Tel: 028 8225 0058
www.grovehillanimaltrust.org

GSD 2000 Rescue & Re-home
Tel: 01242 680 052
www.gsd2000.com

Hull Animal Welfare Trust
Tel: 01430 423986
www.hullanimalwelfare.co.uk

K9 Focus
Tel: 01769 560928
www.k9focus.co.uk

Labrador Rescue Kent & Borders
Tel: 01634 666 419
www.labrescuekent.co.uk

Labrador Welfare
Tel: 0114 266 1756
www.labradorwelfare.org

Last Chance Hotel
Tel: 01209 281159
www.lastchancehotel.org

Lancashire German Shepherd Rescue
Tel: 01772 633860
www.lancsgsdrescue.co.uk

MADRA
Tel: 00 353 86 814 9026
www.madra.ie

Maxi's Mates
Tel: 07808 839594
www.maxismates.org

Oldies Club
Tel: 08445 868 656
www.oldies.org.uk

Our Special Friends
Tel: 01284 810220
www.ourspecialfriends.org

PAWS (Ireland)
Tel: 052 53507
www.paws.ie

Pro Dogs Direct
Tel: 07766 021465
www.prodogsdirect.org.uk

Rainbow Rescue
Tel: 07709 714546
www.rainbowrehoming.com

Rottweiler Welfare Association
www.rottweilerwelfare.co.uk

Scottish Staffordshire Bull Terrier Rescue
Tel: 01463 831271
www.staffierescuescotland.co.uk

Bryony

On a visit to Danaher Rescue Centre in Wethersfield, Essex, Jon Hunt chose Bryony, or rather she chose him. 'She came for a weekend trial visit and stayed with us for just over eleven years. She was gentle, loving and loyal, and she adored our old Labrador Paddy. Bryony was a great help in the house – pulling sheets off the bed and tearing up newspapers for the fire. She was a sock-stealer as well as a heart-stealer. We feel she still walks with us along her secret paths in the woods.'

There in her pen she sat. Fat. Matted fur.
She'd been kept in a garage. She was four.
I almost couldn't meet her gaze.
A wave of shame for humankind.
For broken trust. For wretched days.
This was the second time I'd come
To look at dogs without a home.
We'd just lost our beloved friend:
The shock still fresh in my heart.
We still weren't sure.
'Take her for a walk' I heard.
I jollied her past the pens
And trotted her past her past
Thinking this won't go far;
But as I turned to take her back
She struck out for our car.
Opened the door and she embarked.
Oh thank you – you arrived at last.
And so it was that Bryony came home
So strangely home: so strongly felt
That somehow she'd been here before.
Made friends with Paddy our Labrador:
The two of them lay back to back
Slumbering soundly on the floor.
And oh the pampering she now had!
The sweet shampoos, the walks to slim
The special foods, the cosseting
For such a lady, and for sure
She did deserve it all, and more.
So grateful, peaceful with her past
So happy to be home at last
No longer wary of our garage door.

Siberian Husky Club GB Welfare Scheme
rebecca@shcgbwelfare.org.uk
www.shcgbwelfare.org.uk

Staffie and Stray Rescue
staffiesrescue@gmail.com

Staffordshire Rescue Scotland
Tel: 07594 897338/07880 741428
www.staffordshirerescuescotland.
  org.uk

The Stafford Trust
Tel: 01539 530245
www.sbtrescue.org.uk

Three Counties Dog Rescue
Tel: 01778 440318
www.threecountiesdogrescue.org

Valgrays Border Collie & Animal Rescue
Tel: 01883 624 513
www.valgraysbcrescue.org.uk

West Yorkshire Dog Rescue
www.westyorkshiredogrescue.co.uk

Wirral Animal Welfare Association
Tel: 0151 644 0356

DOGS TRUST REHOMING CENTRES

DOGS TRUST BALLYMENA
Fairview
60 Teeshan Road
Ballymena
Co Antrim
BT43 5PN
Centre open:
12pm– 4pm Saturday – Thursday
Closed on Friday
028 2565 2977
Phone lines:
8am – 8pm Monday – Friday
9am – 5pm Saturday and Sunday

DOGS TRUST BASILDON

Nevendon Road

Wickford

SS12 0FH

Centre open:

12pm – 7.30pm Monday, Tuesday, Thursday and Friday

10am – 4pm Saturday and Sunday

Closed on Wednesday

01268 535 050

Phone lines:

8am – 8pm Monday – Friday

9am – 5pm Saturday and Sunday

DOGS TRUST BRIDGEND

Court Colman

Pen-Y-Fai

Bridgend

Mid Glamorgan

CF31 4NG

12pm – 4pm Tuesday and Thursday – Sunday

12pm – 7.30pm Monday

Closed on Wednesday

01656 725219

Phone lines:

8am – 8pm Monday – Friday

9am – 5pm Saturday and Sunday

DOGS TRUST CANTERBURY

Radfall Road

Chestfield

Near Whitstable

Kent

CT5 3ER

Centre open:

12pm – 4pm Friday – Tuesday

12pm – 7.30pm Thursday

Closed on Wednesday

01227 792 505

Phone lines:

8am – 8pm Monday – Friday

9am – 5pm Saturday and Sunday

DOGS TRUST DARLINGTON

Hill House Farm

Sadberge

Co Durham

DL2 1SL

Centre open:

12pm – 4pm Friday – Tuesday

12pm – 7pm Thursday

Closed on Wednesday

01325 333 114

Phone lines:

8am – 8pm Monday – Friday

9am – 5pm Saturday and Sunday

DOGS TRUST EVESHAM

89 Pitcher's Hill
Wickhamford
Evesham
WR11 7RT
12pm – 4pm Friday – Monday
12pm – 4pm Tuesday – Thursday
Closed on Wednesday
01386 830 613
Phone lines:
8am – 8pm Monday – Friday
9am – 5pm Saturday and Sunday

DOGS TRUST GLASGOW

315 Hamilton Road
Uddingston
Glasgow
G71 7SL
Centre open:
12pm – 4pm Thursday – Monday.
12pm – 7pm Tuesday
Closed on Wednesday
0141 773 5130
Phone lines:
8am – 8pm Monday – Friday
9am – 5pm Saturday and Sunday

DOGS TRUST WEST LONDON

Highway Farm

Harvil Road

Uxbridge

UB9 6JW

Centre open:

12pm – 4pm Monday, Thursday and Friday

12pm – 7.30pm Tuesday

11am – 4pm Saturday and Sunday

Closed on Wednesday

01895 453930

Phone lines:

8am – 8pm Monday – Friday

9am – 5pm Saturday and Sunday

DOGS TRUST ILFRACOMBE

Hazeldene

West Down

Ilfracombe

North Devon

EX34 8NU

Centre open:

12pm – 4pm Thursday – Tuesday

4.30pm – 7.30pm Wednesday

01271 812 709

Phone lines:

8am – 8pm Monday – Friday

9am – 5pm Saturday and Sunday

DOGS TRUST KENILWORTH

Honiley

Kenilworth

Warks

CV8 1NP

Centre open:

12pm – 4pm Saturday, Sunday, Monday, Tuesday, Thursday

12pm – 7.30pm Wednesday

Closed on Friday

01926 484 398

Phone lines:

8am – 8pm Monday – Friday

9am – 5pm Saturday and Sunday

DOGS TRUST LEEDS

Woodlands Farm

York Road

Leeds

LS15 4NL

Centre open:

12pm – 4pm Friday – Monday

12pm – 7.30pm Tuesday and Thursday

Closed on Wednesday

0113 281 4920

Phone lines:

8am – 8pm Monday – Friday

9am – 5pm Saturday and Sunday

Donna

Apart from being adept at breaking and entering, Donna is secretly 'very quiet and a born worrier', according to owners Cindy and Tony Hilling. She enjoys her walks and feels safe in the field and paddock near her home, but on the whole prefers to stay indoors. She is terrified of thunderstorms and 'generally finds the world a scary place'. She came from Romford Greyhound Owners' Association.

Donna, dog. Escape artiste.
Cat burglary considered.
Can manage mortise locks with teeth
But bolts are better sliddered.

No job too small, like oven door,
Fridge freezer, bag or bin.
No gate so great I can't get out
Or hatch I can't get in.

I'm black, elusive, quiet and neat
And won't grass out a chum.
Donna.com. Apply on line
But watch your bloomin' bum.

DOGS TRUST LOUGHBOROUGH

Hill Farm

Wide Lane

Leicestershire

LE12 6SE

Centre open:

12pm – 7pm Monday – Wednesday

12pm – 4pm Friday – Sunday

Closed on Thursday

01509 880 070

Phone lines:

8am – 8pm Monday – Friday

9am – 5pm Saturday and Sunday

DOGS TRUST MANCHESTER

Parkway

Denton

Manchester

M34 3SG

Centre open:

12pm – 7.30pm Monday, Tuesday, Thursday and Friday

10am – 4pm Saturday and Sunday

Closed on Wednesday

0161 337 3600

Phone lines:

8am – 8pm Monday – Friday

9am – 5pm Saturday and Sunday

DOGS TRUST MERSEYSIDE

Whiston Lane

Huyton

Liverpool

L36 6HP

Centre open:

12pm – 4pm Thursday – Tuesday

Closed on Wednesday

0151 480 0660

Phone lines:

8am – 8pm Monday – Friday

9am – 5pm Saturday and Sunday

DOGS TRUST NEWBURY

Plumb's Farm

Hamstead Marshall

Newbury

Berks

RG20 0HR

Centre open:

12pm – 4pm Thursday – Monday

12pm – 7.30pm Tuesday

Closed on Wednesday

01488 658391

Phone lines:

8am – 8pm Monday – Friday

9am – 5pm Saturday and Sunday

DOGS TRUST SALISBURY

45 Amesbury Road

Newton Tony

Wiltshire

SP4 0HW

Centre open:

12pm – 4pm Friday – Monday

12pm – 7.30pm Tuesday and Thursday

Closed on Wednesday

01980 629634

Phone lines:

8am – 8pm Monday – Friday

9am – 5pm Saturday and Sunday

DOGS TRUST SHOREHAM

Brighton Road

Shoreham by Sea

West Sussex

BN43 5LT

Centre open:

12pm – 4pm Thursday – Monday

12pm – 7.30pm Wednesday

Closed on Tuesday

01273 452576

Phone lines:

8am – 8pm Monday – Friday

9am – 5pm Saturday and Sunday

DOGS TRUST SHREWSBURY

Roden Lane Farm

Telford

Shropshire

TF6 6BP

Centre open:

12pm – 4pm Friday – Tuesday

12pm – 7.30pm Thursday

Closed on Wednesday

01952 770225

Phone lines:

8am – 8pm Monday – Friday

9am – 5pm Saturday and Sunday

DOGS TRUST SNETTERTON

North End Road

Snetterton

Norfolk

NR16 2LD

Centre open:

12pm – 4pm Thursday – Tuesday

Closed on Wednesday

01953 498377

Phone lines:

8am – 8pm Monday – Friday

9am – 5pm Saturday and Sunday

DOGS TRUST WEST CALDER

Bentyhead

West Calder

West Lothian

EH55 8LE

Centre open:

12pm – 4pm Friday – Monday and Wednesday

12pm – 7.30pm Thursday

Closed on Tuesday

01506 873459

Phone lines:

8am – 8pm Monday – Friday

9am – 5pm Saturday and Sunday

WOOD GREEN ANIMAL SHELTERS (DOGS)

GODMANCHESTER

Wood Green, The Animals Charity

King's Bush Farm

London Road

Godmanchester

Cambridgeshire

PE29 2NH

Phone: 0300 303 9333

Email info@woodgreen.org.uk

HEYDON

Wood Green, The Animals Charity

Highway Cottage

Chishill Road

Heydon

Hertfordshire

SG8 8PN

Phone: 0300 303 9333

Email info@woodgreen.org.uk

BLUE CROSS RESCUE AND REHOMING CENTRES (DOGS)

BLUE CROSS WEST MIDLANDS, BROMSGROVE

Address: Wildmoor Lane, Catshill, Bromsgrove B61 0RJ

Phone: 0300 777 1460

11am – 4pm Thursday – Tuesday

Closed on Wednesday

BLUE CROSS BURFORD, OXFORDSHIRE

Address: The Blue Cross, Shilton Road, Burford OX18 4PF

Phone: 0300 777 1987

11am – 4pm Thursday – Tuesday

Closed on Wednesday

BLUE CROSS REHOMING CENTRE, SUFFOLK

Address: Bourne Hill, Wherstead, Ipswich IP2 8NQ

Phone: 0300 777 1480

11am – 4pm Thursday – Tuesday

Closed on Wednesday

Amber

The Collie Cross

Amber arrived at Dogs Trust Shoreham branch (01273 452 576) after her owner was taken into care. She was shy and wary of strangers in case they hurt her, so she needed time to build up trust, and an adult-only home with no other dogs. Her back legs were stiff so she couldn't walk that far, but 'you would need to be able to throw her tennis ball for her to fetch'. She dreamt of having her own garden to potter around in. Luckily, after reading Amber's poem opposite, Michaela Smith came to Shoreham to offer her a home. Amber slimmed down, got fit, visited the high Welsh hills and has been loved enormously ever since.

I dream of the high Welsh hills
And the sheep scattered and scurrying
And I am worrying at their heels
Rounding them, driving them
Hurrying into the pen.

I dream that my limbs are young again
And I'm running as fast as the gull flies
For the fox with the sun in his eyes
Who has not seen me.

I dream of the owner I had
And the sad day we parted
When I was brought here broken-hearted
Scared and suspicious
Bidding dreams goodbye.

I know there may never be
A second chance for me
Though I am gentle with the trusted
Grateful for the days I've had
Glad of the days to come
And yet I dream of a home.

BLUE CROSS REHOMING CENTRE, HERTFORDSHIRE

Address: Kimpton Bottom, Hitchin SG4 8EU

Phone: 0300 777 1490

11am – 4pm Thursday – Tuesday

Closed on Wednesday

BLUE CROSS REHOMING CENTRE, LEWKNOR, OXFORDSHIRE

Address: London Rd, Lewknor OX49 5RY

Phone: 0300 777 1500

11am – 4pm Thursday – Tuesday

Closed on Wednesday

BLUE CROSS REHOMING CENTRE, SOUTHAMPTON

Address: Bubb Lane,

West End, Southampton SO30 2HL

Phone: 0300 777 1530

11am – 4pm Thursday – Tuesday

Closed on Wednesday

BLUE CROSS REHOMING CENTRE, THIRSK

Address: Parklands, Station Road,

Topcliffe, Thirsk YO7 3SE

Phone: 0300 777 1540

11am – 4pm Thursday – Tuesday

Closed on Wednesday

BLUE CROSS TIVERTON ADOPTION CENTRE

Address: Tiverton Adoption Centre,

Chilton Gate, Tiverton EX16 8RS

Phone: 01884 855291

11am – 4pm Thursday – Tuesday

Closed on Wednesday

BREED RESCUE via THE KENNEL CLUB

The Kennel Club publishes its own directory listing the many breed rescue organisations where you can locate a pedigree dog for adoption as well as other useful contact information. For a copy of the directory please email pam.hill@thekennelclub.org.uk

GREYHOUND TRUST BRANCHES

For branch details please go to the Greyhound's Trust website:

www.greyhoundtrust.org.uk

SCOTLAND

Edinburgh

Fife

Scottish Borders

West Scotland

NORTH EAST

Darlington

Durham

East Riding

Humber

Northumberland

North Yorkshire

Pelaw Grange

....

NORTH WEST

Cumbria – South Lakes

Lancashire

Merseyside

Sheffield

West Cumbria

West Yorkshire

....

WEST MIDLANDS

Dudley

Hall Green

Oxford

Perry Barr

Rugby & Coventry

Shropshire

Wolverhampton

....

EAST MIDLANDS

East Midlands

Leicestershire

Northampton

Nottingham

....

EAST OF ENGLAND

East Anglia

Eastern Counties

Kings Lynn

Mildenhall

Peterborough – Brambleberry

Suffolk

Yarmouth

....

SOUTH WEST AND WALES

Cornwall

Dorset & Somerset

Honiton

North Cornwall

North Devon

South Wales

Swindon

West Wales

....

LONDON AND SOUTH EAST

Brands Hatch

Brentwood

Canterbury

Dunton

Harlow

Meopham

Bishops Stortford

Jersey

Portsmouth

Waltham Abbey

Wickford

Willow

The Lurcher

I met Willow, now brimming with health, at a gardening gift shop called Summerhouse in Monks Eleigh, where her owner Emma Cook was working. 'Willow had been handed in to Ipswich Police, starved almost to the point of death. Covered in fleas and sores and unable to stand because she was so emaciated, she was taken to Lily Lurcher's Rescue Centre to Hadleigh Vet Practice, where a very kind nurse sat with her all night and named her Willow. Now hopefully my beautiful girl has a long happy life ahead of her.'

The bundle of bones was handed in.
It was still a dog, though it could not stand:
A brindle, very young.
It did not know the men in blue
Who took its body in their van
To Lily Lurcher's rescue home.
It did not know or understand
The vet who put it on a drip
Or recognise the steady hand
That pressed its pulse or held its head.
What registered that night
Was that a kind nurse, sitting by
Said that she should not die without a name
So Willow she became;
And Willow's ebbing blood began to flow
And Willow's misty mind began to grasp
And Willow's frame began to fill
Breathing in love of life until
A small abandoned heap of bones
Found out a future bright and new:
A Summerhouse, an owner who adores,
Fine food, fun, fleece beneath her paws.
So Willow may give hope to you:
For if a dog as delicate as she
Could rise up from a bag of bones
To grace us all, what might you be?

RSPCA ANIMAL CENTRES AND BRANCHES

For branch details please go to the RSPCA's website:
www.rspca.org.uk

Aberconwy

Alton, Haslemere & Petersfield

Anglesey (Ynys Mon)

Balham & Tooting

Barnsley & District

Basingstoke & Andover

Bath & District

Bedfordshire North

Bedfordshire South

Blackpool/North Lancs

Bolton

Bournemouth & New Forest
    Chiltern

Bournemouth, New Forest &
    District

Bradford & District

Brecknock & District

Bridlington, Driffield & District

Bristol & District

Bromley & District

Buckinghamshire South

Burton-on-Trent

Bury Oldham & District

Cambridge & District

Cambridgeshire Mid East

Canterbury & District

Cardiff & District

Carmarthenshire

Central, West & North East
    London

Ceredigion

Cheltenham & East
    Gloucestershire

Cheshire (Altrincham)

Chesterfield & North Derbyshire

Chiltern

Clwyd & Colwyn

Cornwall

Coventry, Nuneaton & District

Craven & Upper Wharfedale

Crewe, Nantwich & District

Croydon, Crystal Palace &
    District

Cumbria North & East

Cumbria West

Danaher Animal Trust

Darlington & District

Derby & District

Doncaster, Rotherham & District

Durham & District

East Berkshire

East Norfolk

Enfield & District

Essex Havering & Harold Hill

Essex Mid, Brentwood, Chelmsford & District

Essex North East

Essex North West

Essex South West

Essex South, Southend & District

Finchley, Golders Green, Hendon & District

Furness & Barrow

Fylde

Glamorgan North & East

Gloucester City & District

Goole & District

Guildford & District

Gwent

Halifax, Huddersfield & District

Hants & Surrey Border

Harrogate & District

Herefordshire

Hertfordshire East

Hillingdon, Slough, Windsor, Kingston & District

Hull & East Riding

Isle of Wight

Kent - Ashford, Tenterden & District

Kent - Folkestone & District

Kent - Isle of Sheppey

Kent - Isle of Thanet

Kent - North West

Kent - West

Kidderminster & District

Lancashire East

Leeds, Wakefield & District

Leicestershire

Lincolnshire East

Lincolnshire Mid & Lincoln

Lincolnshire North & Humber

Lincolnshire North East

Liverpool

Llys Nini (Covering Mid & West Glamorgan)

London East

London South East

Macclesfield, South East Cheshire & Buxton

Manchester & Salford

Medway West

Mid Sussex & Eastbourne

Middlesbrough, South Tees & District

Middlesex North West

Milton Keynes & North Bucks

Montgomeryshire & Radnor

Newbury & District

Newcastle & North Northumberland

Norfolk West

North Devon

North Somerset

North Teesside & District

North Wiltshire

Northallerton, Thirsk & Dales

Northamptonshire

Northumberland West

Norwich & Mid Norfolk

Nottingham & Notts

Nottinghamshire East

Nottinghamshire West

Oxfordshire

Pembrokeshire

Peterborough & District

Plymouth & South West Devon

Poole & East Dorset

Potters Bar, Hatfield & Barnet

Preston & District

Purley, Caterham & District

Radcliffe Animal Trust

Reading With Oxon Border

Richmond, Twickenham & Barnes

Rochdale & District

Rugby

Scarborough

Sheffield

Shropshire

Solent

South Cotswolds

South East Somerset

South West Somerset

South Wiltshire & District

South, East & West Devon

Southport, Ormskirk & District

Stafford, Wolverhampton & District

Staffordshire North

Stockport, East Cheshire & West Derbyshire

Stort Valley

Stourbridge & District

Suffolk East & Ipswich

Suffolk East Coast

Sunderland, Hartlepool & South Tyneside

Surrey East

Surrey Epsom & District

Surrey Sutton & District

Surrey Woking & District

Sussex Brighton & East
  Grinstead

Sussex Chichester & District

Sussex East & Hastings

Sussex North

Tameside & Glossop

Tunbridge Wells & Maidstone

Walsall

Warrington, Halton & St Helens

Warwickshire South & East

West Dorset

West Gwynedd

West Suffolk

Westmorland

Wigan, Leigh & District

Wiltshire-Mid

Wimbledon & District

Wirral & Chester

Worcester &
  Mid-Worcestershire

Wrexham District & Deeside

York & District

Sparky

There's a dog in a kennel over there
Bang out of order.
He's one of those Jack Russells –
He's a mad marauder.
He says he's full of energy – his name is Sparky.
I said you'll never find a home
With that malarkey.
He's got no manners – shows us up
At Darlington Dogs Trust.
He thinks he's being cheeky
But he's not – he's boisteruss.
I know what I would do with him
But staff here, they're too gentle.
I'd stick a fuse up his behind
And light it, as he's mental.

Splash

There's a dog in a kennel over there
Named Splash. Someone should train him
And make that little monster mind
Before I brain him.
He's one of those Jack Russell tykes:
Done as he liked – you know the story.
Terriers are terrors – they're all muck or
    glory.
Try to look big, behave like bombs –
They're hell, those.
All up and down and in and out
Like fiddlers' elbows.
I know what I would do with him
But staff here, they're too nice.
I'd give him Splash –
I'd flush him down the loo, that's
    my advice.

These little terrors are to be found (in separate kennels) at Dogs Trust Darlington branch. Sparky 'is a cracking dog but he can be a little boisterous at times. He would like an adult-only home and a calm, confident owner who will not be phased by cheeky terrier behaviour.' Splash 'is a little dog, but no one seems to have told him that. He is a great character but he has been used to getting his own way a lot. Training staff here will be happy to advise on settling him in.' (Call Claire on 01325 335 952).

No Name

You'll never love me either: let me go
Back to the cast-off kennels whence I came.
Back with the losers whining on death row.
Don't even bother giving me a name.
There I shall not be beaten, starved or burned.
There I shall not be scared by hearts of stone.
I can brave out that last shot now I've learned
Nothing awaits me worse than I have known.
Humans are masters. They are Number One.
Dogs must accept their fate and not complain.
Just seven days of grace and I'll be gone:
Never to trouble humankind again.

NATHAN
PEARSON